COUPE PAPERS ON PUBLIC ECONOMICS **1**

George E. Peterson, General Editor

Fiscal Federalism and Grants-in-Aid

Edited by
PETER MIESZKOWSKI
and
WILLIAM H. OAKLAND

THE URBAN INSTITUTE
Washington, D.C.

THE URBAN INSTITUTE is a nonprofit research organization established in 1968 to study problems of the nation's urban communities. Independent and nonpartisan, the Institute responds to current needs for disinterested analyses and basic information and attempts to facilitate the application of this knowledge. As a part of this effort, it cooperates with federal agencies, states, cities, associations of public officials, and other organizations committed to the public interest. The Institute's research findings and a broad range of interpretive viewpoints are published as an educational service.

The papers included in this book were prepared under the auspices of the Committee on Urban Public Economics and are here published under the joint sponsorship of that Committee and The Urban Institute. The papers reflect the views of their authors and do not necessarily reflect the views of The Urban Institute, its Trustees, or its Sponsors.

Participants in the First Semiannual Conference of the Committee on Urban Public Economics

Howard H. Chernick
Department of Health, Education, and Welfare

Paul N. Courant
University of Michigan

William A. Fischel
Dartmouth College

Ann Friedlaender
Massachusetts Institute of Technology

Edward M. Gramlich
University of Michigan

Bruce W. Hamilton
Johns Hopkins University

Harold M. Hochman
City University of New York

Robert P. Inman
University of Pennsylvania

Marvin B. Johnson
University of Wisconsin

Helen F. Ladd
Harvard University

Julius Margolis
University of California, Irvine

Martin C. McGuire
University of Maryland

Peter Mieszkowski
University of Houston

Dick Netzer
New York University

William H. Oakland
Ohio State University

Wallace E. Oates
Princeton University

Mancur L. Olson
University of Maryland

Janet Pack
University of Pennsylvania

Rudolph G. Penner
American Enterprise Institute

George E. Peterson
The Urban Institute

Robert D. Reischauer
Congressional Budget Office

Jerome Rothenberg
Massachusetts Institute of Technology

Daniel L. Rubinfeld
University of Michigan

Mahlon Straszheim
University of Maryland

T. Nicolaus Tideman
Virginia Polytechnic Institute

Roger J. Vaughan
Citibank

William S. Vickrey
Columbia University

Richard Wagner
Virginia Polytechnic Institute

William C. Wheaton
Massachusetts Institute of Technology

Michelle J. White
New York University

FOREWORD

With this volume, the Committee on Urban Public Economics and The Urban Institute launch a new publication series, entitled "Papers on Public Economics." The purpose of the series is to relate research in economics and kindred disciplines to current issues in domestic public policy.

For the past 12 years, the Committee on Urban Public Economics (COUPE) has convened twice-yearly meetings of academic researchers to present research in progress and subject it to critical review. The Committee's permanent membership consists primarily of public finance and urban economists, but the research presented has ranged well beyond the traditional confines of these disciplines.

For the past 11 years, The Urban Institute has conducted analysis in support of federal and state-and-local policy choices. When COUPE decided in 1977 that it wished to focus its analytical research more squarely on current domestic policy issues, therefore, it was natural for the two organizations to join their efforts. Under the present format, each COUPE meeting centers around a single area of policy concern. Several research papers are prepared and presented for discussion. The papers in revised form will be published in this series, with summaries of discussion where appropriate.

Four volumes in the series are to be published in 1979. In addition to this first volume on fiscal federalism and grants-in-aid, the volumes will treat, respectively, new developments in regional economics, recent efforts to combine legal and economic analysis, and the operations of public sector labor markets. Volumes will appear at six month intervals thereafter.

Financial support from the Ford Foundation and the public finance research program of the Office of Policy Development and Research of the Department of Housing and Urban Development are gratefully acknowledged.

William Gorham
President
The Urban Institute

June, 1979

CONTENTS

ACRONYMS USED IN THIS VOLUME

ACIR	Advisory Commission on Intergovernmental Relations
AFDC	Aid to Families with Dependent Children
BLS	Bureau of Labor Statistics
CD	Community Development
CDBG	Community Development Block Grant
CETA	Comprehensive Employment and Training Act
CSA	Community Services Administration
DPE	District Power Equalizing
FIRE	Fire, Insurance, and Real Estate
FY	Fiscal Year
HUD	(U.S. Department of) Housing and Urban Development
LES	Linear Expenditure System
LMA	Labor Market Area
LPW	Local Public Works
OLS	Ordinary Least Squares
PEP	Public Employment Program
PWIP	Public Works Impact Program
SEO	Survey of Economic Opportunity
SIC	Standard Industrial Classification
UDAG	Urban Development Action Grant
WIC	Women, Infants, and Children program

INTRODUCTION

Peter Mieszkowski and William H. Oakland

The papers in this volume were first presented at a COUPE conference on the theory and measurement of the effects of federal grants to state and local governments. One of the main themes, or issues, of the conference was the phenomenon of the "flypaper effect" (money sticks where it hits). This effect has been identified through empirical work which demonstrates that, contrary to some theoretical work, nonmatching grants stimulate public spending by an amount substantially greater than increases in other income or resources of the community.

The first two papers in the volume, by Paul Courant et al. and Wallace Oates, bear directly on the empirical finding that a dollar of unmatched aid results in a 45 cent increase in public spending, while the marginal propensity to spend on local public goods out of income is estimated to be about .10. Both papers present models that make essentially the same point, namely that the existence of the flypaper effect can be rationalized if the electorate (the median voter) misperceives the true marginal cost of local public goods and uses the *average* cost of public services to estimate marginal cost. The average cost to the community is lower than marginal cost because of the existence of nonmatching grants.

Courant, Gramlich and Rubinfeld also consider a case where public expenditures are controlled by public employees (they are the median voters). They find that, in this situation, grants will lead public employees to overconsume public goods, but will not affect the wage rate in the public sector.

Martin McGuire's paper consolidates earlier work (1975, 1978) that he has done on grants. This original work should have a significant impact on the theory and estimation of the effects of grants. McGuire postulates that in practice, grants are difficult to classify in terms of price or income components because grantee government can, by a variety of means, change the effective matching requirement (in contrast to the legal matching rate). McGuire, by postulating a Stone-Geory linear expenditure system for local expenditure, is able to estimate the substitution across different public services categories and between public and private goods expenditures. He is able, under certain identifying assumptions, to estimate the proportion of grants converted into fungible resources, the marginal propensity to tax local resources, and the proportion of fungible grants returned as tax reduction. McGuire estimates the flypaper effect to be very large as only 15 percent of the grants are returned in tax reductions.

Marvin Johnson, in his paper on the response to grants in aid of local school districts in Wisconsin, also finds that there is a substantial flypaper effect. This is an important result and it strengthens the case for the view that community income and intergovernmental grants enter public spending decisions differently.

Johnson in the theoretical section of his paper attempts to rationalize the flypaper effect in the context of the preferences of local governmental bureaucrats who value public services and for whom local tax burdens are a negative good. So local officials like to spend but they don't like to raise taxes. This model is an interesting alternative to the misperception approach to the flypaper effect that is developed in other papers in this volume. But if such a model is to explain the higher spending out of grants, it must explain why a tax reduction is "valued less" by the bureaucrats and by the community than tax increases.

Howard Chernick also uses a bureaucratic model in explaining grants. The key idea in his paper is that bureaucrats, in maximizing their objective function, will price discriminate between communities in allocating a fixed amount of federal grants. How much a community receives in grants will depend on how important its programs are to the bureaucrats and how willing it is to provide matching funds. The matching rates in the grants become endogenous. One reason why this idea is important is its suggestion that communities which are willing to spend more may get more grants. This interpretation is in sharp contrast with the usual finding that communities spend substantially more because they receive grants, which subsidize costs. Chernick tests his model and finds that for Basic Water and Sewer Grants those communities willing to pay higher matching rates were favored in aid received.

The paper by Rudolph Penner is a general appraisal of the system of categorical grants. Penner analyses the grant system in the aggregate and finds that, over time, there has been a pronounced movement towards equality in per capita grants in different states. But the grant system is not strongly equalizing because *both* the five richest and the five poorest states were higher than the national average.

Penner then criticizes the categorical grant system on a number of grounds, among them that many grants are too small to be effective, and that where the grants are not income conditioned the benefits often do not accrue to needy persons. The recommendations of the Ford administration to consolidate many of the categorical grants into block grants are discussed and defended. One of the arguments in favor of consolidation is to give state and local officials more discretionary power in allocating resources to the programs most valued by the local electorate. But the decentralization consideration is also why many liberals are suspicious of consolidation and prefer to maintain centralized control of grants despite the inefficiencies and inequities that may creep into a categorical system.

The volume ends with Roger Vaughan's paper on the appropriateness of the use of federal grants for countercyclical purposes. There are two parts to Vaughan's contribution: in the first, he analyzes the duration and frequency of unemployment and the distribution of cyclical unemployment by sector, industry, occupation, socioeconomic status, and region. More specifically, he analyzes the timing and responsiveness of an industry's employment rate to national conditions.

In the second part of his paper, Vaughan analyzes the distribution of a variety of program effects on different groups, industries, and regions. Special attention is paid to primary and secondary effects. One of Vaughan's principal conclusions is that more than 90 percent of the second-round jobs of public works investment are located outside the labor market of the initial investment.

As organizers of the conference and editors of its proceedings, we are pleased that the final papers represent a fairly comprehensive analysis of the main effects of grants. A number of the papers break new ground and should serve as building blocks for further research.

THE STIMULATIVE EFFECTS OF INTERGOVERNMENTAL GRANTS: OR WHY MONEY STICKS WHERE IT HITS

Paul N. Courant, Edward M. Gramlich, Daniel L. Rubinfeld

The theoretical literature on the impact of intergovernmental grants on state and local fiscal behavior has reached a consensus on some basic propositions. According to this theory, the form in which grant assistance is given is very important in predicting the effect of the grant on local public spending. Nonmatching grants are assumed to alter the income available to jurisdictions without altering the relative price of public goods, and are hence assumed to have an effect on local spending similar to that of any other change in private income in the community. Matching grants, on the other hand, cause relative prices to change and thus are found to stimulate more spending per dollar of grant than nonmatching grants.[1]

Empirically, one of these predictions has passed the statistical test and one has failed. The generally confirmed result is that matching grants stimulate more spending per dollar of grant than do nonmatching, revenue-sharing types of grants. Regarding the nonconfirmed hypothesis—that nonmatching grants have spending effects similar to those of other changes in private income—the preponder-

---

1. A good summary of this theory can be found in Wilde (1971).

ance of evidence is that nonmatching grants stimulate much more local spending per dollar of grant than does income going to private citizens within the community. The obvious reason for this phenomenon, which we term the "flypaper effect" (money sticks where it hits), is that bureaucrats and politicians find it easier to avoid cutting taxes when the government receives revenue-sharing monies than they do to raise taxes when some exogenous event raises the income of the community.[2]

The fact that the standard theory of intergovernmental grants has been only partially supported by empirical studies suggests that some modifications to the theory may be in order. In this paper we make two. The first uses orthodox, median-voter assumptions—that the median voter is a private employee taking all wages and prices as given—and shows why even in this case the tax price and spending effects of nonmatching grants and changes in private income may not be identical. The economic rationale for the flypaper effect hinges on the inability of voters to perceive the true marginal price of public expenditures when nonmatching grants are present. Finding this economic rationale of course does not preclude an additional political rationale, but it helps to improve the relevance of the economic theory of grants. The second modification follows the logic of the first, except that we now investigate tax price and spending behavior for the case where some voters belong to the public (rather than private) sector and may possess sufficient power to determine public employee wage rates and output levels.

These two amendments to the traditional theory are developed in a model of an economy with two types of governments—an exogenous federal government and an endogenous local government—and just one type of grant, consisting of nonmatching aid of a fixed dollar amount. The model distinguishes between private and public sector employees, analyzing the optimizing behavior of both.

In the first section of the paper the formal assumptions for both the private and public employee models are presented. The second section uses the private employee model to examine the utility-maximizing behavior of private sector employees when all prices and wages are taken as given and develops our economic rationalization of the flypaper effect. The third section then deals with the public employee case, this time distinguishing between real and nominal

---

2. This empirical literature has been summarized by Gramlich (1977).

flypaper effects because wages may not be exogenous. The final section gives a few concluding observations.

The Formal Assumptions

Consider first a model of community behavior in which the median voter is in the private sector. This private employee is assumed to maximize a utility function whose arguments are private consumption C_p and public output, represented simply by public employment (E_g) following standard accounting conventions. Private consumption goods are bought on a national market at a fixed price (P), and are also produced by the private sector workers in the community (E_p) according to a production function that is homogenous of degree one in E_p. All income earned in the community is assumed to be wage income, earned either by public employees who are compensated at a fixed money rate (W_g) or by private employees compensated at the money wage (W_p), fixed by the homogeneity of the production function and the fact that goods prices are fixed.

The total labor force in the community (E) is the sum of private and public employees:

$$E = E_p + E_g. \tag{1}$$

Total money income earned in the community (W^*E), the gross tax base for both the federal and local government, is the sum of wage income earned by workers in both sectors

$$W^*E = W_p E_p + W_g E_g, \tag{2}$$

where W^* is a wage index.

In the first case (pp. 8–16) we consider the optimization of private employees who choose their desired levels of C_p and E_g, taking W_g, W_p, and P as given. Since W_g is fixed, public employees will be unable to negotiate higher wages and we assume that there will be no incentive for private taxpayers to migrate. This means that the total labor force in the community can be viewed as fixed.[3] However, there could still be an effect of changes in E_g on W^*E through the reallocation of

---

3. Assume for the sake of simplicity that high public sector wages are the only cause of private sector migration. We have dealt with this issue in more detail in an earlier paper where we use models of this sort to examine the real and nominal level of government spending. See Courant, Gramlich, and Rubinfeld (1979).

labor between lower and higher wage sectors. As long as the wage differential is small, however, this effect will be minor and it seems reasonable to expect that private voters will not take account of it in their maximizing calculus. Accordingly we assume that atomistic private voters will treat W^*E as given, despite the fact that general equilibrium shifts in W^*E will be incorporated into the final solution of the model.

In the second case (pp. 16–20) we consider the situation in which public employees have sufficient political-bargaining strength to actually set their own wages. As a result, W_p and P are taken as given but W_g is variable. Then private employees are allowed to migrate out of the community in response to monopolistic public employee behavior. As a result, E can become a negative function of W_g, with the gross tax base varying both through the direct impact on E and the indirect impact of compositional shifts. Public employees are assumed to be aware of these aggregate effects, and thus will incorporate assumptions about changes in W^*E in their maximizing calculus.

The local government must always balance its budget. This is accomplished by the levy of a proportional income tax at a rate which equates income tax revenue plus grant revenue with the level of total public expenditure $(W_g E_g)$ in the community. However, the federal government need not balance its budget and its exhaustive expenditures are assumed to have no impact on local decision making. The federal government influences community behavior by assessing proportional income taxes at the rate t and giving close-ended nonmatching grants of amount B.[4]

Private Employee Optimization

Private sector employees are assumed to maximize utility, subject to the constraint that their expenditures on the consumption good (PC_p) plus their expenditures on public goods at the tax price P_p

---

4. Since we are not forcing the federal budget to be in balance and not treating federal exhaustive expenditures explicitly in the model, we also ignore the fact that the local community must make a federal tax contribution for federal grants. Simply assume that these grants are financed either by a change in exhaustive expenditures or the federal deficit, with no effect on local utility, or that grants are net of the federal tax contribution. Johnson and Tomola (1977) show how the tax contribution effect can be worked into a model of local expenditures.

sum to their income net of federal taxes. Assuming for the moment that the only source of income is wage income, net income is simply $W_p(1 - t)$. The private employee then maximizes

$$U_p = U_p'(E_g, C_p) \tag{3}$$

subject to

$$W_p(1 - t) = PC_p + P_p E_g. \tag{4}$$

The general solution is the familiar condition that the marginal rate of substitution be equal to the relative price of the public good:

$$\frac{U_1'}{U_2'} = \frac{P_p}{P}, \tag{5}$$

where the subscripts of U' denote partial derivatives.

With a proportional income tax, the tax price of public goods that a private sector employee faces will be the net cost of a unit of public goods times the employee's locally taxable share of community income net of federal taxes.[5] Recalling that the net cost of a unit of public goods is W_g, and that nonmatching grants at level B add to community income, the *average* tax price is then

$$P_p = \frac{W_p(1 - t)W_g}{W^*E(1 - t) + B}. \tag{6}$$

Substituting (6) into (4) yields the general expression for the budget constraint as it might be viewed by the private employee:

$$W_p(1 - t) = PC_p + \frac{W_p(1 - t)W_g E_g}{W^*E(1 - t) + B} \tag{7}$$

To examine the effect of grants on local spending, assume that initially $t = 0$ and $B = 0$, and that federal grants at the level B are financed through federal tax rate t which leaves net spendable resources of the community, $W^*E(1 - t) + B = W^*E$, constant.[6] In standard grant theory analysis this type of shift would leave community spending on public output unaffected and there would be no flypaper effect.[7] But in the approach taken here, there can be two

---

5. This was the definition used in Peterson (1973) and Rubinfeld (1977).

6. We make this assumption to simplify the exposition. Unless otherwise stated, the results derived in this section hold in general.

7. See Oates (1972), chap. 3, appendix B, for a good discussion.

separate effects on E_g:

i) since in the short run the private employee will feel that his/her disposable income had decreased (W_p is fixed but t is increased), the perceived individual budget constraint will involve a loss of income equal to tW_p, and this income effect will lower E_g (assuming that E_g is a normal good);

ii) since the numerator of (6) has declined and the denominator has remained constant, the average tax price of public output will fall. If voters are not able to see that the true marginal price of public output is unchanged, this price effect will raise E_g.

There are, in other words, two misperceptions here, one involving income and one involving price. If the voter is laboring under both misperceptions, the net of these two offsetting influences on E_g would appear to depend on the relative strength of the income and price effects. But this is not so. When we take explicit account of the fact that the net spendable resources of the community have remained constant, the income misperception is eliminated and the remaining price misperception will cause public employment and expenditures to increase.

A graphical presentation of our argument is shown in figure 1. Assume for convenience that the private employee is the median voter in the community and has the usual choice between public and private goods. As before, assume that the federal government has no revenue-sharing program and no federal taxes, so that line MR, the maximum value of private consumption for the consumer, equals W_p. The initial equilibrium for money public expenditure levels is at $W_g E_g{}^0$ ($E_g{}^0$ is denoted by 0 on the graph). Then the central government introduces a revenue-sharing grant to the community of B, simultaneously taxing all income earned in the community at rate t such that aggregate community spending power, $W^*E(1-t) + B$, is left unchanged at W^*E. Standard grants analysis would predict that this consumer and the community will remain at point 0 because there has been no change in either income or relative prices at the margin for the community. But this may not be the case. In the first instance the consumer is likely to think that the price of public output has fallen and that his income has been reduced to $W_p(1-t)$ by the federal income tax. He will face the budget constraint represented by line segment ST, and will optimize at point V choosing public expenditures of E_1 (this would be the case when public expenditures demands

Figure 1

(assume $P = 1$)

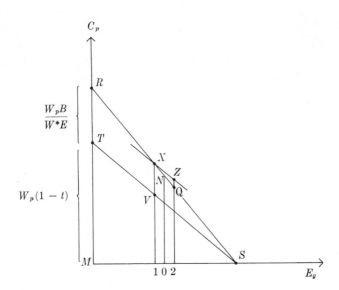

are inelastic and the income effect outweighs the substitution effect). But along ST the consumer is only spending his after-tax private income, not his share of the revenue-sharing grant, and if all consumers do likewise, the local government will run a surplus.

The surplus arises as follows. Given that expenditures have been set at level 1, the line segment $1X$ represents that portion of community resources available for private consumption by the private-sector employee. (Recall that RS represents the true trade-off between public and private expenditures.) However, the private employee has calculated his private consumption to be equal to line segment $1V$. The result, when the government actually spends $W_g E_g^1$, is an unexpected surplus of VX dollars per private employee. In the first instance local officials will presumably compute this surplus at the actual level of public expenditures and mail this consumer his share, a check in the amount of VX.

Since the price of public goods to the consumer has not changed with the return of the surplus, the private employee will then view his constraint line as XZ and vote, say, for expenditure level 2. At this higher expenditure level the government will run a deficit of an amount equal to ZQ for this particular employee. As a result the original rebate check will be reduced and a new budget line drawn. This process will eventually converge towards an equilibrium. The equilibrium point will lie on line RS, the true community resource constraint line, and will be the point of tangency between an indifference curve and a price line parallel to XZ and ST. We will see that at this final equilibrium the rebate the consumer receives will be less than his federal tax payment by the complement of the proportion of income spent on the public sector. Moreover, since community resources are the same as before the policy change, the private good price remains at P, the price of public goods faced by the individual is reduced, and the final level of expenditures must necessarily increase. The trade of revenue sharing for private incomes has *raised* public spending and resulted in what would appear to empirical researchers to be a flypaper effect.[8]

This result can be obtained mathematically if we solve to find the surplus or incremental income, ΔY, to be returned to the private employee so that the final equilibrium occurs at a point which marks his expenditure choice, given income $(W_p + \Delta Y)(1 - t)$ and facing a relative price of public output P_p/P. The incremental income is determined from the community resource constraint which arises in the standard case in which all revenue-sharing funds are allocated to consumers who then make their public or private choice. Since BW_p/W^*E represents the employee's share of revenue sharing money, it follows that

$$W_p \left(1 - t + \frac{B}{W^*E}\right) = PC_p + \frac{W_p W_g E_g}{W^*E} \tag{8}$$

where $W_g W_p/W^*E$ is the true marginal cost of public output. But the

---

8. At this point we can return to a statement made above and say that any compositional effects on W^*E from (2) will also influence the final community-wide equilibrium by adjusting the community-wide resource constraint line. For Walrasian reasons, the local government will find it possible to mail a check for the maximum amount of private consumption individual households can engage in at any level of E_g without unbalancing their own budget. If changes in E_g influence the aggregate constraint line, therefore, these shifts will be incorporated in the rebate checks.

employee's optimization involves the following budget constraint

$$(W_p + \Delta Y)(1 - t) = PC_p + \frac{W_p(1 - t) W_g E_g}{W^*E}.$$ (9)

Combining (8) and (9) to solve for ΔY, we find that (using the fact that $tW^*E = B$):

$$\Delta Y = \left(\frac{W_p B}{W^*E}\right)\left(1 - \frac{W_g E_g}{W^*E}\right)\left(\frac{1}{1 - t}\right)$$ (10)

Thus, the increment to after tax income, $\Delta Y(1 - t)$, is equal to the private employee's share of nonmatching grants, less the fraction of that share spent on public output. If all income in the community is devoted to public output, the income increment is zero. If none of it is spent on public output (and the federal government permits the community to keep the grant), disposable income increases by the employee's share of the grant. Since the increment to income will also be subject to federal taxation, the community-resources constrained income of the employee becomes

$$Y_p(1 - t) = (W_p + \Delta Y)(1 - t) = W_p(1 - t)$$
$$+ \frac{W_p B}{W^*E}\left(1 - \frac{W_g E_g}{W^*E}\right).$$ (11)

Now we are in a position to prove that an increase in t and B which leaves community resources constant will always increase the desired level of public output, E_g. To see this, note that the effect of such a change on $Y_p(1 - t)$ and $P_p E_g$ is of equal magnitude and sign when E_g is held constant. That is, for $d(tW^*E) = dB$ and E_g fixed (from equations [11] and [6]),

$$\frac{dY_p(1 - t)}{d(tW^*E)} = \frac{-W_p W_g E_g}{(W^*E)^2} = \frac{dP_p}{d(tW^*E)} E_g.$$ (12)

Equation (12) implies that the change in disposable income is just equal to the change in expenditure necessary to purchase the initial C_p and E_g pair, implying that the initial bundle is attainable under the changed tax price and disposable income. But if the initial pair was an equilibrium under the initial prices—i.e., if equation (5) held— then it cannot be an equilibrium under the changed price ratio. In particular, if dt is positive, the relative price of public goods will have fallen and private employees will demand more public goods than they did at the initial price ratio. Of course, the increase in demand for public goods will engender a decrease in $Y_p(1 - t)$ through (11), and thus the equilibrium level of E_g which is demanded will fall between the initial level and that which would be demanded if $Y_p(1 - t)$ remained at the level associated with the initial level of E_g. But in essence, balanced (federal) budget changes in t and B alter perceived relative prices while leaving real consumption opportunities unchanged.

The difference between standard analysis and that given above is that standard analysis assumes away all illusions. The aggregate omniscient political authority is assumed to know that the trade of revenue-sharing and federal taxes does not change relative prices for the community at large, and is assumed to respond accordingly. But in real life there is not one aggregate decision maker but a host of voters who, to the extent that they are guided by economic considerations, would presumably be aware only of their own average tax prices—not the relative price structure facing the community at the margin. As long as the government does not incorporate the revenue-sharing grant in locally taxable income, voters will vote for higher levels of public expenditures.[9] In terms of the graph, the government can eliminate this misinformation only by restoring the initial price line RS. The obvious way of doing this would be to give consumers the full prorated revenue-sharing grant, making $(W_p + \Delta Y)(1 - t) = W_p(1 - t + B/W^*E)$, and then assessing tax shares on this basis

$$P_p' = \frac{W_p(1 - t + B/W^*E)W_g}{W^*E(1 - t) + B} = \left(\frac{W_p}{W^*E}\right)W_g \qquad (13)$$

so as to make individual budget constraints equal to (8) in the standard analysis and then to emasculate the price effect. Incidentally, it is clearly in the community's (perhaps not the bureaucrat's)

---

9. It is conceivable that over time voters will learn that the level of $Y_p(1 - t)$ is systematically and negatively correlated with E_g, and thus learn that their true budget constraints are given by equation (8) and line RS in figure 1. But such learning can only be expected to take place if there are repeated changes in t and B, and if voters keep records on the effects of such changes and undertake statistical analyses of the relationship between their disposable income and the behavior of the public sector in response to such changes. To say the least, the information requirements placed upon individuals in such a scenario make it implausible.

interest to make this tax price correction, for the switch between revenue sharing and taxing has altered neither tastes nor the boundary of the opportunity set and hence expenditure level 2 is clearly not an optimum. Any deficiencies in the standard analysis are, in other words, descriptive but not normative.[10]

We can also consider the implications of the preceeding analysis if local revenues are raised by property taxation rather than income taxation. Here the extent to which capitalization occurs is the key issue. If the value of nonmatching grants is capitalized into property values, then the local tax base will rise by the amount of such grants, while the local level of disposable income will fall by the amount that federal taxes are increased to finance the nonmatching grants. The numerator of (13) is unchanged and there is no price effect of the type we have considered.[11] To the extent that nonmatching grants are not fully capitalized, the "price-illusion" analysis presented above is appropriate, as some portion of local resources will not be locally taxable. Again, in the short and medium run, incomplete capitalization, and hence the flypaper effect, would seem to be a plausible result.

Finally, we should try to assess the quantitative importance of the flypaper rationale we have identified. The disparity between the estimated marginal propensity of public spending with respect to private income and unconditional transfers is on the order of $.40: if a community raises public spending by x when private income rises $1.00, it raises public spending by $x + $.40$ when unconditional transfers rise $1.00 (here the value of x depends on the taste for public and private goods, which is assumed to be different across communities). In the experiment we examine here, the federal government

---

10. In the simple case we have used here to illustrate the problem, an alternative way of making the correction would be to assign tax shares equal to W_p/W^*E, ignoring federal taxes and transfers altogether. That will not work whenever the change in income tax revenues does not equal the change in revenue sharing grants, however. Then (13) must be used.

11. Note that even with complete capitalization, an increase in federal taxes used to finance a nonmatching grant such that community resources are left constant will not be perfectly analogous to the standard case unless each household's annual imputed rental gain from property is just equal to its loss of disposable income. Since this condition will never be met in practice, such a policy change would in general change the distribution of income in a community. If there are income effects on the demand for public goods, this would lead to a change in demand—although the sign of the change is uncertain.

conducts a balanced-budget change that leaves the community resource constraint unaffected, but which does pivot the price line around the initial point. If the reduction in the perceived price is .1 (B/W^*E goes from 0 to .1) and the price elasticity of demand for public expenditures with community resources held constant is .5, W_gE_g/W^*E will rise by .05. Say that initially W_gE_g/W^*E equals .2, as it does in many communities. The new level of W_gE_g/W^*E is .21, the change in public spending is $.01W^*E$, and the change in B is $.1W^*E$. Hence this change will appear as a difference in the marginal propensity to consume unconditional transfers over private income of as much as .1 for certain communities. We cannot, nor would we want to, explain the entire observed flypaper effect with this phenomenon, but in certain communities with a high level of B, a high level of public spending, and strong price elasticities, these orders of magnitude show that the phenomenon could be a significant force.[12]

Public Employee Optimization

To this point we have examined grant theory under the assumption that the private sector median voter implicitly determined public employment levels. Now we show how the results change when public employees have varying degrees of electoral or bargaining power. We make three sets of assumptions: (a) that public employees have sufficient electoral power to determine their own employment levels; (b) that employees have sufficient bargaining power to determine their own money wages; (c) that employees have enough power to determine both public employment and wages.

In the first case, public employees control (either through voting or through other political processes) the level of public output, but public wages are given exogenously. The median public employee voter then maximizes

$$U_g = U_g'(E_g, C_g) \tag{14}$$

12. In a companion paper whose content we were not aware of until the first draft of our own was completed, Wallace Oates explains a much larger share of flypaper effect through a phenomenon that sounds suspiciously like ours. There is a difference, however. Oates' voters misperceive the marginal price even more that ours do—they would consider it line TN in figure 1. We reduce the perceived price by just the reduction in perceived average tax prices; Oates reduces it by the share of expenditures paid for by unconditional grants ($[W_gE_g - B]/W_gE_g$ in our notation). Oates also does not have the community resource constraint built in. See Oates in this volume.

subject to

$$Y_g = PC_g + P_g E_g \tag{15}$$

with

$$P_g = \frac{W_g^2(1-t)}{W^*E(1-t)+B}. \tag{16}$$

The solution to this system is essentially the same as before, except that public wages play a dual role—being a component of both the income of public employees and the price they have to pay for public goods. If basic taste parameters are the same, public employees will have a higher demand for public output when $W_g > W_p$ and the income effect outweighs the substitution effect, and a lower demand when the substitution effect outweighs the income effect. As before, there is a flypaper effect when the public employee receives as income some portion of the revenue-sharing grant as long as that grant is not included in the computation of this tax price.

Now consider the second case in which public employees have no control over output, but do have sufficient bargaining strength to raise their wages above that of private employees.[13] To illustrate the nature of the results, we make the strong assumption that public employees can set W_g, and examine the partial equilibrium results when E_g is fixed.

The solution to this case turns out to hinge on the elasticity of the overall tax base, W^*E, with respect to W_g. As long as E_g is fixed, a rise in W_g will increase the money income earned by the public sector, $W_g E_g$, proportionately. But if there is intercommunity migration in response to the rise in W_g, resulting in a fall in $W_p E_p$, the overall tax base, $W_p E_p + W_g E_g$, will not rise in proportion to W_g and may even fall. If we define

$$\eta = \left(\frac{dW^*E}{dW_g}\right)\left(\frac{W_g}{W^*E}\right) \tag{17}$$

as the elasticity of this tax base with respect to the public wages, the above remarks imply that η is strictly less than one and may even be negative.

---

13. Studies of public sector wages indicate that this may be the case for many urbanized areas with strong unions. See Smith (1977) and Ehrenberg and Goldstein (1975) for the general proposition, and Horton (1973) for a description of how it might have already happened in New York City.

The first order condition when E_g is held fixed can be found simply by maximizing C_g with respect to W_g in equations (14)–(16). Using the same assumptions as in the previous section regarding the treatment of rebate checks

$$C_g = W_g\left\{1 - t + \frac{B}{W^*E}\left(1 - \frac{W_g E_g}{W^*E(1 - t) + B}\right)\right\}$$

$$- \frac{W_g(1 - t)W_g E_g}{W^*E(1 - t) + B}$$

or   (18)

$$C_g = W_g\left(1 - t + \frac{B}{W^*E}\right)\left(1 - \frac{W_g E_g}{W^*E(1 - t) + B}\right).$$

If public employees know the size of their tax and revenue-sharing change, they know also that both the aggregate spendable resources and $(1 - t + [B/W^*E])$ will not be affected by the federal policy changes, though of course they must also worry about the fact that increases in W_g could reduce the community tax base W^*E if $\eta < 0$. Their optimal solution is given by

$$\frac{W_g E_g}{W^*E(1 - t) + B} = \frac{1}{2 - \eta}.$$ (19)

If η, the elasticity of the overall tax base with respect to public wages, equals zero, these wages will be set so that the aggregate net public sector wage bill equals just one-half of total community spendable resources. As employees increase their wage beyond this level, the increase in the local tax rate necessary to finance the further wage increases is so great that employees' command over consumption goods actually declines. If $\eta < 0$, the share of resources devoted to the public sector is further reduced by employees' fear of losing tax base when they raise their wages; while $\eta > 0$ the same consideration will raise their wage bill. But as long as $\eta < 1$, which it clearly is as long as $W_p E_p$ does not increase, (19) will be a maximum for public employees and will insure that the public wage bill is less than the level of total output.

Since the optimization condition is stated in terms of the total public wage bill, as the public employee work force expands, increases in W_g must be paid to additional workers, who cost more in terms of necessary tax increases. Hence there is an inverse correlation between the size of the public employee work force and the wage that each can extract. Regarding grants, there is no flypaper effect in this situation. No matter how the government sets tax shares, the employees are assumed to know that aggregate resources are held equal by the federal change, and to set wage policy to take the appropriate fraction.

We note one other interesting feature of (19). If there were no federal taxes or grants, then local tax rates on all income would equal $1/(2 - \eta)$. If the federal government decides to increase its own taxes without a compensatory increase in nonmatching grants, the local public sector is left to take $1/(2 - \eta)$ of a smaller remainder, so that the combined local-federal tax rate is larger than $1/(2 - \eta)$. Generalizing, in a hierarchical federal system with strong employee unions each of which is setting wages on the basis of income left over after the higher level governments take their share, the combined tax rate for all levels of government could get quite large—asymptotically approaching unity in all cases and realistically being well in excess of one-half even when η is close to zero.

The final case where public employees set both wage and employment levels is a composite of the first two. The wage first-order condition (given E_g) is equation (19), and the employment first-order condition (given W_g) is found by maximizing (14) subject to (18). Since public employee households gain their revenue-sharing checks but are not taxed on them at the local level, the employment first-order condition leads them to overconsume public goods, as in the private sector flypaper case. But since optimal wage behavior is set by (19) and is independent of the origin of the community's tax base, there is in effect no *nominal* flypaper effect. Hence the simultaneous solution of the two first-order conditions is that *real* expenditures are larger than before the federal policy change (and larger than if tax prices were computed optimally), that nominal expenditures are exactly the same, and that public sector wages are *reduced* by the so-called flypaper effect. In the private sector optimization case, the unadjusted tax price leads voters to overconsume real and nominal government expenditures; but in the public sector case the same phenomenon leads to overconsumption of public goods and less exploitation of the private sector through high public-sector wage levels. In a welfare sense, the flypaper effect made the private sector worse off when they were determining employment levels and better off when public employees were determining both wage and employment levels.

Implications

In this paper we try to amend the standard theory of intergovernmental grants by inquiry into the mechanism by which grant-induced changes in community prices and incomes are actually transmitted to individual voters. In the first half of the paper we find an economic rationale for a well-known empirical puzzle in the grant literature—that a dollar of nonmatching aid seems to stimulate a good deal more local public expenditures than a dollar change in private community income, despite the fact that both should have had exactly the same effect on community-wide relative prices and incomes. The rationale is that in order for the nonmatching grant neutrality to hold, local officials must take the grants into account in computing tax shares, an action that seems quite unlikely. If this is not done, there will be a relative price effect for nonmatching grants which will stimulate expenditures more than private income increases. All of this is, of course, not to deny that there could be other, more powerful, political reasons for the empirical puzzle in addition to the economic rationale we have given.

In the second section of the paper we extend this reasoning to the case where public employees are the median voters. These employees are allowed, successively, control over expenditure levels, wage levels, and both together. Incorrectly viewed relative prices will lead public employees to overconsume public goods just as with their private sector counterparts, but will not affect their wage behavior or the size of the public budget in nominal terms. Hence when public employees control employment as well as wages, the incorrect relative prices will actually aid the private sector—leading to the same sized budget in nominal terms but greater levels of real expenditures and lower levels of public wages.

REFERENCES

Courant, Paul N.; Gramlich, Edward M.; and Rubinfeld, Daniel L. 1979. Public Employee Market Power and the Level of Government Spending. Forthcoming in *American Economic Review*.

Ehrenberg, Ronald G., and Goldstein, Gerald. 1975. A Model of Public Sector Wage Determination. *Journal of Urban Economics* 2: 222–45.

Gramlich, Edward M. 1977. Intergovernmental Grants: A Review of the Empirical Literature. In Wallace E. Oates, ed., *The Political Economy of Fiscal Federalism*. Lexington, Mass.: Lexington Books, 219–39.

Horton, Robert D. 1973. *Municipal Labor Relations in New York City: Lessons of the Lindsay-Wagner Years*. New York: Praeger.

Johnson, George E., and Tomola, James D. 1977. The Fiscal Substitution Effect of Alternative Approaches to Public Service Employment Policy. *Journal of Human Resources* 12: 3–26.

Oates, Wallace E. 1972. *Fiscal Federalism*. New York: Harcourt, Brace, Jovanovich.

Peterson, George E. 1973. The Demand for Public Schooling. Urban Institute Working Paper No. 1207–28. Washington, D.C.

Rubinfeld, Daniel L. 1977. Voting in a Local School Election: A Micro Analysis. *Review of Economics and Statistics* 59: 30–42.

Smith, Sharon P. 1977. Government Wage Differentials. *Journal of Urban Economics* 4: 248–71.

Wilde, James A. 1971. Grants-in-aid: The Analytics of Design and Response. *National Tax Journal* 24: 573–84.

LUMP-SUM INTERGOVERNMENTAL GRANTS HAVE PRICE EFFECTS

Wallace E. Oates

This paper seeks to resolve an emerging inconsistency: the existing theory of intergovernmental grants suggests that unconditional grants have only income effects, with the implication that they will provide only a modest stimulus to budgetary expansion, while empirical studies find a much greater expansionary impact than can be rationalized in terms of a pure increase in income. This apparent inconsistency is of some importance, for it obscures the perspective we should take on basic programs, such as federal revenue-sharing and certain state grants to local authorities. If, for example, the theory is correct, then revenue-sharing becomes simply a veil for a federal tax cut to individuals. Several years ago, Bradford and Oates produced a set of sufficient conditions for an unconditional intergovernmental grant to be fully equivalent, in both its allocative and its distributive effects, to a set of lump-sum grants made directly to the individuals who constitute the collectivity. This proposition, although hedged by a number of important restrictions, seemed fairly powerful and compelling. In particular, it suggested that an additional dollar of

ACKNOWLEDGMENT.   I am grateful to David Bradford, Sharon Bernstein Megdal, Kenneth Rosen, and the members of COUPE for a number of helpful comments on an earlier draft of this paper. Financial support for this research was provided through a grant to the Princeton University Economics Department from the Sloan Foundation. Wallace E. Oates, Princeton University.

lump-sum grants to a government should have roughly the same expansionary impact on public expenditure as a dollar increase in the private income of that jurisdiction.

However, empirical work indicates otherwise. In a recent survey of empirical studies of intergovernmental grants, Gramlich (1977) concludes that the "work to this point strongly suggests that revenue-sharing is not a veil for tax cuts—that it does make an appreciable difference in the pattern of expenditures whether the federal government disburses untied aid to state and local governments or makes untied tax cuts benefiting individuals" (p. 230). Although the findings vary considerably among studies, they nearly all imply a marginal propensity to spend from lump-sum grants well in excess of the $.05 to $.10 range of estimated responses in state-local public expenditure to a one dollar increase in private income. The Gramlich and Galper study (1973), for example, estimates that an additional dollar of unconditional aid to state and local governments induces, on average, a 43 cent increase in their spending. Gramlich observes, "The results are so striking that the field could well use more theory . . . on whether and under what conditions the standard indifference-curve, utility maximization analysis had better give way to a variant more cognizant of political realities" (p. 230).[1]

This paper is a direct response to Gramlich's challenge. It sets forth a simple model of local budgetary choice consisting of output-maximizing local officials constrained by voter preferences. The model generates what is at first sight a rather surprising phenomenon: lump-sum intergovernmental grants have the effect of simply reducing the price of local output (resulting in a movement along the demand curve). In contrast, an increase in private income shifts the demand curve in the usual way. I have deliberately kept the model extremely simple (but, I think, fairly realistic within these limits) to focus on this fundamental asymmetry, for it is this kind of asymmetry that is implied by the empirical evidence.

---

1. An alternative response to this apparent inconsistency between theory and measured behavior is embodied in the intriguing paper in this volume by Howard Chernick. Chernick contends that at least certain forms of nonmatching grants have quite important incentive effects. More specifically, grant administrators, through negotiation, seek (and typically obtain) a substantial commitment of resources from recipients to supplement whatever aid is given. This suggests that much of what has been treated as lump-sum grants for purposes of empirical analysis may, in fact, have important *implicit* matching provisions.

The Model

In brief, the model[2] postulates that local government seeks to maximize output. One can envision a local school board that attempts to expand the curriculum in local schools and to enrich its quality. The local authority must, however, "sell" its program and the associated budget to the electorate. The demand functions of the electorate thus become a constraint on the determination of the local budget. In particular, I shall employ the standard median-voter proposition in the following way: local officials set output at the highest level consistent with the demand of the median voter. To motivate this assumption, consider again a local school board which presents to the electorate a proposed budget on which voters must indicate their approval or disapproval by a simple yes or no. If the proposed budget is rejected, then a process is set in motion (perhaps, but not necessarily, involving a subsequent vote) which will result in a somewhat reduced level of expenditure. In this case, all those who wish a budget equal to, or larger than, that proposed by the school board will vote yes. Those who prefer a smaller budget may vote no with the prospect of a lower level of spending and taxes. The school board, to guarantee itself of majority support for its proposal, sets its budget equal to the median of the voters' preferred budgets. A proposal in excess of this runs the risk of rejection.[3]

Voters make their decisions on the basis of two pieces of information: the level of output (Q) and the associated tax liability (T), which implies that voters know only the tax-price (Q/T), not necessarily the true cost, of providing the proposed level of services. Imagine once again the local school board taking to the voters an annual proposal for a program of school services and a property-tax levy to finance the program. What happens in this model is that intergovernmental grants allow the local authority to provide a given

---

2. The model developed in this section is quite similar in spirit to that in Courant et al. in this volume. The magnitudes of the implied responses to grants are, however, quite different.

3. More formally, the "reversion level" to which the budget adjusts in the event of rejection is of crucial importance. If, for example, a rejection of the board's proposal entails a drastic cut, some of those who would have preferred a budget only slightly less than that on the ballot may vote yes. Thus, somewhat paradoxically, a very low reversion level may permit local authorities to get assent to a larger budget than otherwise. For a careful treatment of all this, see Romer and Rosenthal (1977).

level of services at a lower tax-price to the voters; this is the source of the price effect.

Somewhat more formally, the model can be expressed in terms of the following system of six equations:

$$B = Q \tag{1}$$

$$B = T + R_o \tag{2}$$

$$P = \frac{B - R}{B} = \frac{T}{Q} \tag{3}$$

$$Q_d = Y_o^\alpha \, P_m^\beta \tag{4}$$

$$P_m = \gamma P \tag{5}$$

$$Q_s = Q_d, \tag{6}$$

where:

B = Total public expenditure on the service,

Q = Level of output of the service (subscripts d and s refer to quantity demanded and quantity supplied),

T = Locally raised tax revenues,

R_o = Intergovernmental grants received (exogenously determined),

P = Tax-price per unit of output (where subscript m refers to the tax-price of the median voter),

Y_o = Level of private income (exogeneously determined).

Equation (1) states that the size of the budget is equal to the level of output; here I assume that output is provided at constant cost with units defined so that cost per unit is one.[4] Equation (2) indicates that whatever part of the budget is not financed by (exogenously determined) intergovernmental revenues must be met by local tax receipts. Equation (3) defines the tax-price to the community; note that the community's *perceived* price is the *average* tax cost per unit. (More on this soon.) In (4), I assume a simple multiplicative demand function, where the individual voter's demand function for the public

---

4. For purposes of the analysis here, I shall simply assume that local officials provide public services at minimum cost. Alternatively, one could posit that the constant cost per unit includes an element of waste or "fat" in the budget. Either interpretation will generate the asymmetry that is the central concern of this paper.

service depends upon his (given) level of income and his tax-price. The demand function in (4) is that of the median voter who is the point of reference for the analysis; his tax-price, P_m, is assumed in (5) to be some predetermined fraction of P, the tax-price to the community. Finally, equation (6) embodies the assumption of output maximization by local officials: it says that these officials set output at the maximum level that voters can be sure to support by pushing the budget to the largest size consistent with a guarantee of majority assent (i.e., the median of the most preferred budgets). The model consists of six equations and six unknowns and will, in general, produce a solution when private income and intergovernmental grants are given.

Figure 1 depicts this solution. Let D_m represent the demand curve of the median voter. In the case where intergovernmental grants are zero, the tax-price to the median voter is represented by a straight line with a vertical intercept equal to γP_m. Note the effect of a positive lump-sum intergovernmental grant: it shifts γP_m to $\gamma P_m'$ by lowering the tax-price of output. The result is that we move along the

Figure 1

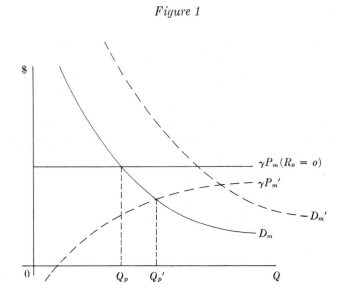

demand curve to a higher level of output, Q_p'.[5] The asymmetry between lump-sum grants and increases in private income is immediately apparent. Increases in income shift the demand curve outward (as illustrated by D_m'), while grants lower the price to the taxpayer-voter and produce a downward movement along his demand curve.

It is, incidentally, unclear whether a one-dollar increase in grants will lead to less, the same, or more public spending than a one-dollar increase in private income. That depends on the price and income elasticities of demand. If we differentiate the system for B with respect to Y and R, we find that:

$$\frac{dB}{dR} = \frac{-\beta T^{-1}}{F} \tag{7}$$

$$\frac{dB}{dY} = \frac{\alpha Y^{-1}}{F} \tag{8}$$

where: $F = \dfrac{1 - \beta(R/T)}{B}$.

For (7) to exceed (8), we require that:

$$\frac{-\beta}{\alpha} > \frac{T}{Y} \tag{9}$$

(i.e., that the ratio of absolute value of the price elasticity of demand to the income elasticity of demand exceed local taxes as a fraction of private income). Existing elasticity estimates (see, for example, Bergstrom and Goodman, 1973) for local services suggest that the value of the left-hand side of (9) is on the order of one-half, which well exceeds the value of the right-hand side. Inserting some typical values for the parameters and variables into (7) and (8), I calculated that $dB/dR \approx .4$ and $dB/dY \approx .1$ which are quite close to actual estimates.

---

5. An admitted difficulty with the analysis is that we have no guarantee that the same person in the before and after situations will be the median voter. It is, thus, not quite legitimate to assume that we are moving along one individual's demand curve, although this may still represent a reasonable approximation. One set of conditions sufficient to guarantee that the median voter doesn't change is that all voters have the same underlying preference functions, that output is financed by a proportional or progressive income tax, and that alterations in the distribution of income are not so large as to change the rank ordering of incomes. This is obviously a very restrictive set of conditions.

None of these computations, of course, should be taken very seriously in such a simplified model. Nevertheless, it's always encouraging to see one's model generate plausible results.

Fiscal Illusion and Voter Behavior

One aspect of this formulation requires further comment. It might appear from equation (6) that the existence of an output-maximizing local authority is superfluous to the model; since the equilibrium output is that demanded by the median voter, it would seem that a voting model is all that is needed. This, however, is not quite true. In fact, the local government uses the grant funds to deceive voters (who possess less-than-complete information about the true cost of output) into agreeing to an excessively high level of output. The marginal cost of output *to the electorate* is unity so that the median voter would prefer, in figure 1, an output of Q_p, irrespective of whether there are grant funds available or not.[6] But what the electorate sees is not a price of unity, but rather a tax-price equal to the fraction of total costs covered by local tax collections; the voter thus uses an average tax-price (which is less than the true marginal cost to him) to decide on levels of output. There is a kind of fiscal illusion in the model, which the local authority operates to its advantage by generating a higher level of services than the electorate would really desire if it had accurate cost information.

This clarifies somewhat the source of the asymmetry in the collective-choice mechanism. Increases in personal incomes to the members of a community are not equivalent, in terms of their budgetary effects, to an equal increase in lump-sum intergovernmental revenues because, although they may generate the same true budget constraint, they do not result in the same *perceived* budget constraint. In general, voter choices will depend on the particular form in which their increase in resources comes.

REFERENCES

Bergstrom, T., and Goodman, R. 1973. Private Demands for Public Goods. *American Economic Review* 63: 280–96.

---

6. This ignores any income effects associated with the grant (which is probably an appropriate assumption, since grant funds disbursed by a higher level of government must be financed by taxes). For a treatment which incorporates explicitly the cost of the grants, see Courant et al.

Bradford, D., and Oates, W. 1971. The Analysis of Revenue Sharing in a New Approach to Collective Fiscal Decisions. *Quarterly Journal of Economics*, 85: 416–39.

Chernick, H. The Economics of Bureaucratic Behavior: An Application to the Allocation of Federal Project Grants. This volume.

Courant, P.; Gramlich, E.; and Rubinfeld, D. The Stimulative Effects of Intergovernmental Grants: Or Why Money Sticks Where It Hits. This volume.

Gramlich, E. 1977. Intergovernmental Grants: A Review of the Empirical Literature. In W. Oates, ed., *The Political Economy of Fiscal Federalism*. Lexington, Mass.: Lexington Books, 219–40.

Gramlich, E., and Galper, H. 1973. State and Local Fiscal Behavior and Federal Grant Policy. *Brookings Papers on Economic Activity* 1: 15–58.

Romer, T., and Rosenthal, H. 1977. Bureaucrats vs. Voters: On the Political Economy of Resource Allocation by Direct Democracy. Unpublished manuscript.

THE ANALYSIS OF FEDERAL GRANTS INTO PRICE AND INCOME COMPONENTS

Martin C. McGuire

For two decades students of local public finance and of fiscal interaction among governments in a federal system have been working to understand and explain the response of local government to federal grants. Over this period of time the growth in federal grants may have outpaced the advance in our understanding of how they work, but progress has not been negligible. Rigorous application of classical demand theory has produced believable estimates of the demand parameters of local behavior. (See especially Gramlich and Galper 1973 and Gramlich 1976.) Prior to this innovation federal grants seemed to be astonishingly stimulative of local fiscal effort (Osman 1966, for instance). Nevertheless the best analyses have often had recourse to ad hoc constructs such as Okun's flypaper "theory," that grant money sticks where it hits.

Evidently the proceedings of this conference indicate a shift in approach to the analysis of local fiscal response, and in particular a closer, more critical examination of the realism of the assumptions behind classical demand theory for describing local government decision making.

[The author is a member of the Department of Economics, the University of Maryland.]

ACKNOWLEDGMENT. Support of the National Science Foundation, GS 33966, is greatfully acknowledged.

In that context, the effect of federal grants on local allocations is to be explained in terms of preferences (local and federal) and resource constraints. But just whose preferences count and whether preference *maximization* captures the behavior of a local bureaucracy is open to question. Similarly, just how federal intervention actually changes the resource constraint faced by local governments is a second question for analysis. Can we assume that the nominal conditions imposed by granting authorities are the same as the effective conditions perceived by the receiving government?

Drawing on earlier work (McGuire 1975 and 1978) this paper has three purposes. First, we summarize the argument that strong reasons exist for suspecting the nominal provisions and restrictions of grant programs; ordinarily these nominal provisions will differ from the effective changes in local resource constraint brought about by a grant; and, it is the *effective* induced resource constraint which governs the local response to grants. Second, we discuss alternative econometric models for distinguishing between nominal and effective changes in the local budget constraints. Third, we summarize the results from estimation of one of those models.

Applicability of the Consumer Demand Model to Local Government Allocation Decision

In order to interpret observed resource allocations on the part of various levels of government one requires a model. Rigorous studies of this problem have depicted local allocation decisions in the classic model of the individual consumer, that is, as maximization of a preference function subject to resource constraints (see especially Gramlich 1969). Our study also will employ a consumer-allocation model, but the classic model will be modified to reflect the peculiarities of the grant system, thus permitting an empirical estimation of how that system operates. Before formulating the model, however, we must address two questions which call into doubt the validity of using it at all.

First, there is doubt that complicated bureaucratic decisions can be represented as conscious, utility-maximization processes. For our purposes we can dispense with the conscious maximization hypothesis, provided we assume that local bureaucracies show consistent responses to price and budget changes. (In the long run, federal intervention may change local attitudes and perceptions of needs as well as the responsiveness of local officials to client demands. These effects are ignored here.) The essential fact that local decisions depend on both preferences and opportunities simultaneously does not necessarily mean utility maximization is the only or best model of local behavior. Other norms such as budget or bureau-maximizing practices should be explored and the empirical method presented in this study should be of use in making such comparisons. A second, more serious, problem is whether grants-in-aid can validly be characterized as price-plus-income changes with the implicit assumption that local governments retain freedom to make marginal allocation choices once grants are introduced into the process. I want to consider this question at length: first, to clarify the behavioral context in which the consumer model can be applied, and second, to argue on theoretical grounds that such a context may well, in fact, obtain.

For some very simple aid mechanisms a grant merely changes price and income. In figure 1, for example, if line *B* shows the local budget before federal grants, line *C* can be used to represent an unconditional grant or a general increase in local resources and therefore a pure income effect. Line *D* represents an open-ended but conditional (or matching) grant as a pure price change; lines *E* and *F* show combinations of simple price and income changes. If the grant system functions in any one of these ways, one can validly explain local allocation choices (assumed to be point *a* in figure 1) in terms of income and prices. Other, more complex grant mechanisms, however, may confront a community not with continuous marginal choices but with a discrete take-it-or-leave-it offer. Figure 2 offers one such example, a fixed-sized categorical grant which requires no matching local funds, but is policed to ensure no reduction in local effort. This device also moves the community from point *b* to *a*, although point *a* is not caused by price-income changes. Note, however, that point *a* would have been the outcome under a marginal choice process for any of an infinite number of multipart pricing offers by federal authorities. For example, a fixed charge of *ed* followed by a price subsidy (shown by line *dca*) would equally have stimulated selection of point *a*. In this case, income and price effects of the federal grant could be identified with the first and second parts, respectively, of the multipart price. (Another multipart price with the same result is price *ec* up to point *c*, followed by price *ca* thereafter.)

Which account is more realistic for describing grant systems? There is probably no single answer to this question, since procedures

Figure 1

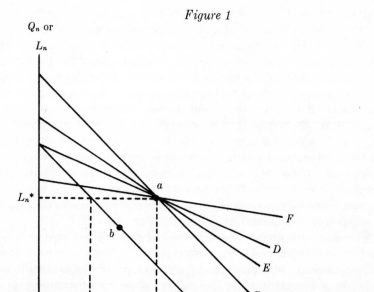

Figure 2

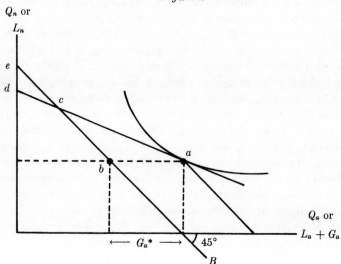

vary among different functional programs and levels of government. But, although we cannot settle the question conclusively, a strong argument can be made in favor of the multipart price, continuous-choice alternative. For example, the grant-in-aid system is embedded in a political process with a large element of bargaining and negotiation; hence there are built-in incentives for striking mutually beneficial bargains. In particular, key provisions of grant programs— such as matching ratios and budget allotments to states and other jurisdictions—are not determined arbitrarily. Rather, they are agreed upon in a process of legislative-executive bargaining. Further, the very intricacy of rules and regulations for grant controls makes them vulnerable to manipulation by local governments. And finally, in many cases local authorities may have perfectly legal options available for defeating the nominal purpose of grants.

Consider, for example, the variety of options which a local authority might exercise to transform conditional, or categorical, grants back into fungible resources. One opportunity to thwart the conditional purpose of a federal subsidy will arise when local leaders can trade the subsidized good on a "market"; for by so doing they will reconvert a conditional subsidy to a general income supplement. Sales of the services of a subsidized public facility (say, water or waste treatment) to another local authority will accomplish this purpose. If direct sales of the subsidized output are physically impossible or legally prohibited, then other indirect forms of exchange may be possible: the local government may possess an equivalent, salable good, or local authorities may convert conditional to unconditional resources—not by selling more or less substitutable goods, but by renting them out or imposing user charges. Alternatively, categorical grants may in effect be traded for general resources through time; where a local government plans to invest in future public capital projects, it may borrow money for present construction, thereby using the federal cost share to reduce future tax loads. Or again, when the benefits of a public facility appear in the form of increased profits to local firms or increased incomes to local citizens, the local government will recover a portion of the subsidy as local taxes. Possibly the greatest opportunity for defeating intended conditional effects occurs in cases where grants are supposed to apply only to increases in local output over current levels. By understating or reducing normal funding to the subsidized programs, by using a project which would be undertaken in any case as the vehicle for securing a matching grant, by redefining budget categories, or by a judicious allocation of overhead costs, local officials may, in effect, convert the grant to a pure income supplement. To the extent that such options are exercised by local government, the nominal legal provisions of grant programs will not reveal the actual change in local opportunities caused by federal intervention.

Three such possible means of converting a conditional matching grant into fungible resources are illustrated in figure three. Figure 3a shows the case when a subsidized good can be resold in a market. A pregrant budget line and nominal open-ended matching grant are shown as lines A and B, respectively. If a limited amount of the subsidized good can be traded back at the market price the true post-grant budget constraint is line C. Whereas the donor (nominally) believes the recipient government has chosen an allocation such as point b, in fact the receiver is able to trade back to point c (the broken line from b to c is assumed to be parallel to the original budget line A, reflecting the assumption that the aided good can be traded back at cost. If aided goods could only be resold at a discount the broken lines should be less steep). Presumably at the level of individual grant programs such a phenomenon will occur when easily marketable commodities like food are subsidized.

Figure 3b shows the effect of a redefinition of program categories. The receiving government receives a nominal open-ended matching grant (line B), but within limits can redefine categories (e.g., school busing which once fell into transportation, police services which once fell into public safety, or recreation services which had stood alone, all now become "education"). The effective postgrant budget constraint is the kinked curve C. While the donor thinks the local government has chosen point b, a redefinition of program categories has, in fact, placed the receiving government at point c.

Figure 3c illustrates the case in which overhead costs from another program are loaded onto the grant-aided program. The pregrant budget line is shown by the kinked line A, the horizontal segment representing overhead or fixed costs for good Q_n. By allocating all these overhead costs to Q_a, a receiving government can alter the effective budget constraint induced by an open-ended grant from line B to line C. The figure as drawn assumes that the donor government will subsidize all of the fixed costs of Q_n (on the mistaken impression that they apply to Q_a) even when no Q_a is produced.

In view of local options for converting conditional to fungible resources, the way to discover the *effective* change in the resource

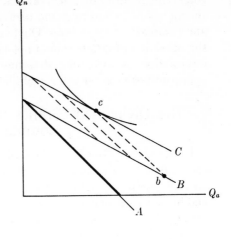

Figure 3a

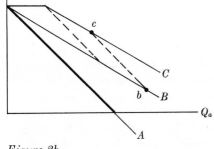

Figure 3b

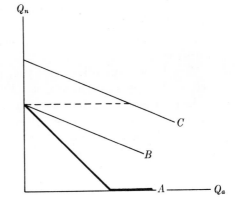

Figure 3c

constraint induced by a federal grant is probably not to sift through the morass of federal rules and regulations concerning matching ratios and enforcement procedures. Obviously, reliable prior information on the operation of grants should not be discarded, but even when such information is available, determination of the changes in local opportunities induced will remain largely a statistical problem.

The Division of Grants into Price and Income Components

I have shown elsewhere (McGuire 1975, 1978) that if we assume conventional price and income effects to explain local allocation then an econometric model can separate and identify the effective price and income components of the grant. Here we recapitulate the idea on the simplifying assumption that all grants received are retained in the public sector. This assumption is relaxed later. Reference is made to figures 1 and 4. We divide the accounting expenditures of a local government into three categories: L_n being expenditures on nonaided functions; L_a being expenditures on the aided function (where both these expenditures are from local resources); and G_a, representing grants received from other levels of government to supplement the aided function. (We shall use L_a, L_n, and G_a to denote dollar expenditures; Q_a and Q_n to denote physical quantities or indices thereof; and p to denote the price of Q_a.) Time-series or cross-sectional data will show a number of observations of realized outcomes for the various local decision units. Figure 4 shows one such observation as a point labeled a. This point implies a local expenditure L_a^* on aided categories, L_n^* on other categories, and a grant of G_a^*. Line B (a 45-degree line) shows how the total observed local government expenditures $(L_a^* + L_n^*)$ might feasibly have been allocated otherwise.

The basic assumption being that the particular combination a was *chosen* by the local government, the question naturally arises as to which budget limitation actually constrained the observed choice. Figure 1 shows four possibilities, all consistent with the observed grant, G_a^*. Corresponding to each of these alternative budget constraints is a different set of local preferences explaining the selection of point a. Line C represents a pure budget-supplementing grant with no price effect; line D, a pure price subsidy with no budget effect; line E, a two-part price consisting of budget supplement plus a price subsidy; and line F, a two-part price consisting of an effective budget reduction plus an over-compensating flat price subsidy.

Since the price and income components of observed grants are unknown, we are ignorant of what combination of the above constraints actually restricted the local decision. Thus we want to formulate federal-local allocations in such a way as to allow statistical tests to reduce this ignorance.

Assuming federal intervention to take the effective form of multipart pricing, the local government will find a portion of the grant to be a fixed cost or revenue supplement. The remainder of the grant is devoted to designated categorical purposes, in accord with some *effective* matching requirement (in contrast to the nominal or legal matching ratio). One can imagine various processes with this result: for example, federal grants purposely might be part categorical, part revenue sharing; federal enforcement procedures might allow a portion of grants to be diverted as revenue supplement; or as argued in the preceding section if federal and local representatives in effect bargain simultaneously for the size of federal grant allotment and for an ex post matching ratio, the effect is equivalent to a multipart pricing system. In any case, the net effect of local options for defeating matching requirements will be reflected in this effective matching ratio. Figure 4 shows the model in detail for the particular hypothetical observation (L_n^*, L_a^*, G_a^*). For illustration we assume that the local public budget line does not shift in as a result of the grant; i.e., we assume zero tax relief. We postulate that G_1, a part of the total grant, is in effect a pure revenue-sharing budget supplement (G_1 may be positive or negative); G_1 is the fixed portion of the multipart price. Total fungible resources available to local officials, that is, the total local government budget B (including G_1) therefore is

$$B = L_a + L_n + G_1. \tag{1}$$

In selecting point a, the local government actually chooses to expend $L_a^* + G_1^*$ of this total budget on Q_a, paying an effective price of

$$p^* = \frac{L_a + G_1}{L_a + G_a} = 1 + \frac{G_1 - G_a}{L_a + G_a} \tag{2}$$

(equal to the slope of its postgrant budget line). The variable p therefore represents the postsubsidy price of the aided category as a percentage of total unit cost. While local officials spend $(L_a + G_1)$ of

Figure 4

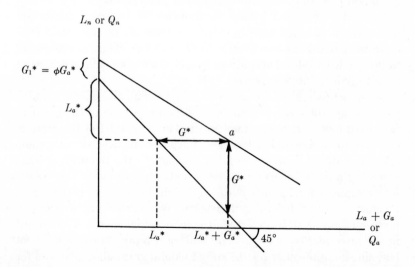

their fungible resources on the aided function, the quantity they receive costs $(L_a + G_a)$. Thus we have broken down the total grant-in-aid into two component parts, G_1, an income component, and $(G_1 - G_a)$, a price change component.

Our basic assumption is that local officials maximize utility at reigning prices subject to their resource constraint—a process generating estimable demand functions which depend systematically on income and prices. Our objective then is to use the variables B and p, just derived, as data in demand estimation. However, while this procedure decomposes a grant into a price and an income changing component, neither component is directly observable. Only the total, G_a, is observable. In order to estimate these price and income changing components some *a priori* relationship must be assumed between them. Three alternatives come to mind. For instance one might assume that the income component G_1 is constant K across all observations. This assumption implies a local budget of $(L_a + L_n + K)$ and a price of $(L_a/[L_a + G_a] + K/[L_a + G_a])$. Alternatively one might assume G_1 is a constant proportion ϕ of G_a, i.e., $G_1 = \phi G$. In this case the resource constraint becomes

$L_a + L_n + \phi G_a$ and the price $[1 + (\phi - 1)G_a/(L_a + G_a)]$. Still another possibility is to assume that ϕ depends on some variable such as the size of the local government (on the theory that big local governments have greater options for switching funds about), with the attendant derived income and price components of the grant. (See McGuire 1975 for more detail.) Obviously numerous other alternatives exist, including the traditional one of assuming $G_1 = G_a$ and a zero price effect.

Bureaucratic Processes and Specification of the Price-Income Components of Grants

In order to estimate statistically the differential price and income effects of federal grants we need to break one observed variable into two unobserved components, G_1, an income component, and p, a price component. Since G_1 and p are not observed, the only way to estimate their separate effects is to make some assumption as to the structural relation between them, or, equivalently, some assumption as to the functional relationships $[G_1 = f(G_a)$ and $p = h(G_a)]$ between each and the observed variable G_a. Whether one chooses one of the alternative assumptions spelled out above, or some altogether different structure, the postulated relation between p and G_1 must of course reflect the fact that price and income changing grant components add up to G_a, the observed total grant. Moreover, and more importantly, any assumption will imply (or be implicitly derived from) some concept of the bureaucratic process through which the federal grant and the local response are "negotiated." More specifically our use of the classical utility maximizing model together with a price-income disaggregation assumes that local decision units choose a point of tangency between their indifference maps and price adjusted budget line. *This assumption in turn entails that the federal government practices some form of price or income discrimination in its grant distribution.* That is, if different local governments receive different total grants, and spend varying amounts of local resources on an aided function, then the effective price subsidy will vary across different receiving governments, so that by implication the federal-local negotiation process involves some type of price discrimination and/or some type of budget-supplementing discrimination among localities. I myself do not find this implication at all anomolous. There is a sizeable literature on how costs should be shared on

Figure 5

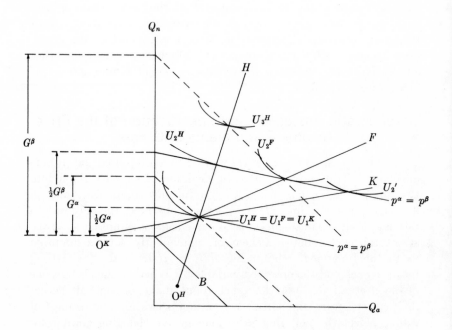

federal-local projects; government agencies do attempt to discriminate among grantees using cost sharing proportions as instruments; and critics such as Schultze (1969) have advocated such policies.

This principle is illustrated in figure 5. The axes Q_a and Q_n having been defined already, line B shows the local public budget before any grant. Suppose that, as a grant is given, none is absorbed as tax relief (there is no loss in generality from this assumption which will be relaxed later in this paper). Assume some value for ϕ, say $\phi = 0.5$, that is, 50 percent of grants are converted into fungible resources. Then the line F shows observed allocation patterns consistent with no price discrimination. That is, ϕ^α for grant G^α is the same as ϕ^β for grant G^β, p^α for grant G^α is the same as p^β for G^β ($\phi^\alpha = \phi^\beta$, $p^\alpha = p^\beta$, $G^\alpha < G^\beta$). Thus if local preferences were as U_1^F, U_2^F, etc., the federal government could put out (or get rid of) larger grants without offering greater price incentives. Suppose, however, local preferences were homothetic with reference to point 0^H as an origin. Then a representative set of indifference curves would be U_1^H, U_2^H, U_3^H, etc., along line H. In this case either price p^β should have to be lowered to induce the local government to absorb the higher grant ($\phi^\alpha = \phi^\beta$, $p^\alpha > p^\beta$; $G^\alpha < G^\beta$), *or* the proportion ϕ should have to increase with G ($\phi^\alpha < \phi^\beta$, $p^\alpha = p^\beta$, $G^\alpha < G^\beta$).

Next, in contrast, suppose the local preferences were homothetic with reference to 0^K as an origin. Then a representative set of indifference curves would be along line K, U_1^K, U_2^K, U_3^K, etc. In this case it would follow that a larger grant could be dispersed at a *higher* price, or a lesser leakage into the fungible category than a small grant would require. The econometric setup to which we turn next allows us to discriminate between these alternative hypotheses. As we will discuss later, the empirical distinction between lines H, F, and K shows up in the estimates of price elasticity.

Econometric Set-Up: The Case of Fixed Proportions between G_a and G_1

The case in which G_1 is some fixed proportion ϕ of G_a, so that $G_1 = \phi G_a$, has been examined in some detail elsewhere. (McGuire 1975, 1978.) Future analysis may of course validate other hypotheses about $G_1 = f(G_a)$; nor is there reason to expect the same hypothesis to be relevant for different programs or different levels of government. Nevertheless the assumption that ϕ is constant across observations seems a reasonable point of departure. In this case one convenient demand system to estimate is the Stone-Geary linear expenditure system.

Expenditures $= pQ = \alpha_0 + \alpha_1$ [Resources] $+ \alpha_2$ [Price]
Substituting for "price" from equation (2) one obtains as a typical equation to be estimated

$$L_a = \beta_a [R_L + \phi G_a] - \phi G_a + \gamma_a (1 - \beta_a)$$

$$\left[1 + \frac{(\phi - 1) G_a}{L_a + G_a} \right] - \beta_a \gamma_y \qquad (3)$$

If we felt sure that our assumption of zero tax relief were valid then R_L ("local" resources) could be taken directly from equation (1). However, since we later will want to check the validity of this assumption we will interpret R_L as local resources available for public *and* private consumption. Using this broader interpretation of the local budget equation (3) follows from maximization of a utility function

$$U = (Y - \gamma_y)^{\beta_y} (Q_a - \gamma_a)^{\beta_a}$$

subject to the resource constraint

$$R_T = R_L + \phi G = Y + p Q_a$$

where R_L = local resources; R_T = total resources; and
$\quad\;\; Y$ = local consumption of private goods.

Equation (3) is a simplified version of more complex linear expenditure systems which we have estimated. Equation (3) however highlights several features of the larger system. First, the structural parameters are determined. In particular the value of ϕ can be solved from the regression coefficients. Second, the matching rate $[G_a/(L_a + G)]$ is evidently correlated with the error term requiring two-stage least-squares estimation with independent instruments or some surrogate. *Third, for G_a and the matching rate to be independently exogeneously determined one must assume as in the previous section that federal authorities control the matching rate as a discriminating instrument. With this assumption both G_a and $[G_a/(G_a + L_a)]$ are set exogenously by the grantor.* Fourth, the effect of an income-supplementing grant ϕG of, say, \$1.00 on local expenditure decisions is assumed to be the same as the effect of \$1.00 more in local resources. (This is the antithesis of the flypaper theory of grants.) And fifth, if a more complex demand function were to be chosen, it should have to be a polynomial in resources, grants, and prices for linear estimation techniques to be used in identifying the crucial parameter. This is the basic reason for using the Stone-Geary system. Other more desirable forms are not estimable. Future work however might well employ nonlinear estimation of, say, constant elasticity demand systems.

Tax Relief Effects of Grants

The flypaper theory of grants says that grant money from a higher level of government is spent entirely on the function for which it is given. At the opposite pole one might suppose fungible grant money is simply added to local resources and reallocated into local public programs at the prevailing marginal tax rate. Equation (3) can be adjusted to test these hypotheses by adding a parameter π as follows:

$$L_a = \beta_a \left[R_L + \pi \phi G_a \right] - \phi G_a + \gamma_a \left(1 - \beta_a \right)$$

$$\left[1 + \frac{(\phi - 1) \ G_a}{L_a + G_a} \right] - \beta_a \gamma_y \qquad (4)$$

This adjustment, while in a sense *ad hoc* allows one to discriminate as between the effects of internal versus external resource growth on local allocations to the aided function. For $\pi = 1$, the fungible component of grants is treated by the local bureaucracy as identical with internal resources. For $\pi = 1/\beta_a$ the flypaper theory fits perfectly; all fungible grants are allocated to the aided category. And for $\pi > 1/\beta_a$ more than the entire fungible component of a grant is allocated to the aided function. Thus, the tax relief effect of \$1.00 in fungible grants becomes $(1 - \pi \beta_a)$ assuming no other local public good. Similarly if a second local public good Q_n is incorporated into the model, the tax relief from \$1.00 in *fungible* grants (i.e., $\phi G_a = $ \$1.00) becomes $(1 - \pi \beta_a - \pi \beta_n)$ where β_n denotes marginal propensity to allocate internal resources to the other local public good, Q_n.

Unfortunately, inspection of equation (3) indicates that our introduction of a differential in local treatment of grants in comparison with internal resources produces an undetermined equation. One escape is to assume a value for some other structural parameter (e.g., let $\gamma_y \equiv 0$). Alternatively one can expand the equation (3) system to incorporate a second aided function. In detailed empirical work, we have in fact opted for this latter alternative.

Some Results from Estimating The Demand for Education

For empirical estimation the foregoing model has been elaborated to incorporate local private consumption plus two local public-good sectors, education (*ed*) and all other or noneducation (*ned*) activities. Local decision makers are assumed to maximize a three-good utility function

$$U = Y^{\beta_y} \left(Q_{ed} - \gamma_{ed} \right)^{\beta_{ed}} \left(Q_{ned} - \gamma_{ned} \right)^{\beta_{ned}} \qquad (5)$$

subject to a resource constraint

$$\text{Total Resources} = \text{Local Resources} + \pi[\phi_{ed}G_{ed} + \phi_{ned}G_{ned}]$$

$$= p_{ed}Q_{ed} + p_{ned}Q_{ned} + Y.$$

This yields two demand equations for local expenditure on education (L_{ed}) and on noneducation (L_{ned}) with coefficients as follows:

L_{ed}	Independent Variable	L_{ned}
Constant	1	Constant
β_{ed}	Y	β_{ned}
$(\beta_{ed}\pi - 1)\phi_{ed}$	G_{ed}	$\beta_{ned}\pi\phi_{ed}$
$\beta_{ed}\pi\phi_{ned}$	G_{ned}	$(\beta_{ned}\pi - 1)\phi_{ned}$
$(1 - \beta_{ed})(\phi_{ed} - 1)\gamma_{ed}$	M_{ed}	$-\beta_{ned}(\phi_{ed} - 1)\gamma_{ed}$
$-\beta_{ed}(\phi_{ned} - 1)\gamma_{ned}$	M_{ned}	$(1 - \beta_{ned})(\phi_{ned} - 1)\gamma_{ned}$

All structural parameters have been defined already except for $M_{ed} \equiv G_{ed}/(L_{ed} + G_{ed})$ and $M_{ned} \equiv G_{ned}/(L_{ned} + G_{ned})$. Technical details of this demand system are given in McGuire (1978). The system was estimated for pooled cross-section time series of the 48 states for the years 1964–71. In order to wash out underlying state differences in preferences, the minimum subsistence consumption parameters were replaced by indices of socioeconomic characteristics, which vary from state to state and from year to year.

Two-stage least squares estimates of this system have yielded a range of results as follows:

Summary of Results

		Range	Best Estimate
Proportion of Grants Converted into Fungible Resources	ϕ	.26 to .76	.74
Proportion of Fungible Grants Returned as Tax Reductions	$[1 - \pi(\beta_{ed} + \beta_{ned})]$	.82 to .02	.15

Summary of Results—Continued

	Range	Best Estimate
Marginal Propensity to Tax Local Resources $\}\beta_{ed} + \beta_{ned}$	.088 to .095	.09
Price Elasticity of Demand for Education (at sample mean)	−.02 to −.15	−.02
Subsistence Per Capita Consumption of Education (at the sample mean)	$153 to $173	$173

Some of these figures are comparable with other studies of local expenditure. For example, a marginal propensity to tax of 9 percent agrees with other studies. On the other hand Gramlich's flypaper captures only 50 percent of grant money while our best estimate is 85 percent. Clearly therefore this model, or at least our estimates of this model, will not lay the flypaper theory to rest. The above estimate of demand price elasticity for education is lower (in absolute value) than others reported, particularly Feldstein's (1975). (Moreover, this estimate was quite unstable.) Of course the estimate of ϕ is unique to this study.

Figure 6 pictures the outcome of our joint preference function (cum price-budget constraint) estimation for the mean community in the sample. The Stone-Geary preference map is defined only over commodities in excess of the minimum "subsistence" consumption bundle. Thus in figure 6 the estimates of γ_{ed} and γ_{ned} determine the origin of the operational preference map. Within this operational region the preference map is Cobb-Douglas homothetic. Figure 6 shows an assumed zero-grant budget constraint for two public goods. The results are most easily pictured for the case of a zero tax-relief effect. Now consider a small grant $G_{ed}{}^0$, and assume $\phi_{ed} = .5$, and $L_{ed} = L_{ed}{}^0$. Point j illustrates this observation. The indifference curve through j is tangent to the price-budget line p^0.

Figure 6

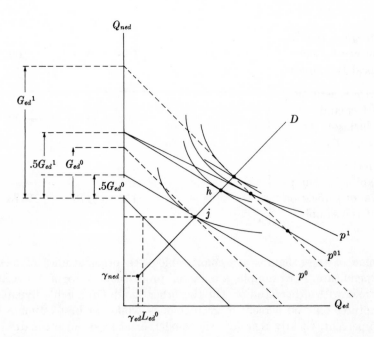

The division of resources at price p^0 would be along line D. Indifference curves along D all have the same slope, p^0. Next, consider a larger grant G_{ed}^1; ϕ_{ed} being constant, equals 0.5. If price p^1 = price p^0 then the price-budget line would be shown as p^{01} parallel to p^0. However p^{01} is tangent to an indifference curve at point h along D. Therefore to absorb the entire grant G_{ed}^1 price must be lowered to, say, p^1. If γ_{ed} were sufficiently negative, the origin of the indifference map would be in the third quadrant and p^1 should have to be higher than p^0. In the linear expenditure system the sign of γ in turn determines price elasticity, for $\gamma > 0$; $-1 < \eta < 0$, and for $\gamma < 0$, $\eta < -1$.

Thus the picture which emerges is that with low price elasticity of demand federal authorities can only exact matching funds from local governments by offering big grant receivers larger price subsidies. This follows from our estimates which suggest (and others do as well though not to the same degree) price inelastic demand. Consequently, it seems that the entire contingent grant apparatus, working against the tide of underlying local preference, is actually not much more than a complicated income transfer mechanism. This conclusion is further borne out by estimates indicating that during the period 1964–71 the proportion of grants converted into fungible resources was increasing (McGuire 1978). Either local officials on the receiving end of education grants increasingly gained the upper hand in federal-local negotiations, or federal enforcement/leverage has declined over the years, or both.

REFERENCES

Bahl, R. W., and Saunders, R. J. Sept. 1966. Variations in State and Local Government Spending. *Journal of Finance.*

Bergstram, T. C., and Goodman, R. P. June 1973. Private Demand for Public Goods. *American Economic Review.*

Borcherding, T. E., and Deacon, R. T. Dec. 1972. The Demand for the Services of Non-Federal Governments. *American Economic Review.*

Ehrenberg, R. G. June 1973. The Demand for State and Local Government Employees. *American Economic Review.*

Feldstein, M. S. March 1975. Wealth Neutrality and Local Choice in Public Education. *American Economic Review.*

Gramlich, E. M. June 1969. State and Local Governments and Their Budget Constraint. *International Economic Review.*

————. Jan. 1976. Intergovernmental Grants: A Review of the Empirical Literature. International Seminar on Public Economics Seminar. Berlin. Reprinted in Wallace E. Oates (ed.), *The Political Economy of Fiscal Federalism.* Lexington, Mass.: Lexington Books, 1977.

Gramlich, E. M., and Galper, H. 1973. State and Local Fiscal Behavior and Federal Grant Policy. *Brookings Papers on Economic Activity,* vol. 1.

Inman, R. P. 1971. Towards an Econometric Model of Local Budgeting. *National Tax Association Papers and Proceedings.* Columbus, Ohio.

McGuire, M. C. May, 1973. Notes on Grants-in-Aid and Economic Interactions among Governments. *Canadian Journal of Economics.*

————. 1975. An Econometric Model of Federal Grants and Local Fiscal Response. In W. E. Oats (ed.), *Financing the New Federalism,* Washington, D.C.: Resources for the Future.

————. Oct. 1978. A Method for Estimating the Effects of a Subsidy on the Receiver's Resource Constraint. *Journal of Public Economics,* vol. 10.

McGuire, M. C., and Garn, H. Feb. 1969a. Problems in the Cooperative Allocation of Public Expenditures. *Quarterly Journal of Economics,* vol. 60.

————. Dec. 1969b. The Integration of Efficiency and Equity Criteria in Public Project Selection. *Economic Journal.*

Oates, W. E. 1972. *Fiscal Federalism.* New York: Harcourt-Brace-Jovanovich.

O'Brien, T. March 1971. Grants-in-Aid: Some Further Answers. *National Tax Journal*.

Ohls, J. C., and Wales, T. J. Nov. 1972. Supply and Demand for State and Local Services. *Review of Economics and Statistics*.

Osman, J. W. Dec. 1966. The Dual Impact of Federal Aid on State and Local Government Expenditures. *National Tax Journal*.

Pidot, G. B. May 1969. A Principal Components Analysis of the Determinants of Local Fiscal Patterns. *Review of Economic Statistics*.

Pogue, T. F., and Sgontz, L. G. June 1968. The Effects of Grants-in-Aid on State and Local Spending. *National Tax Journal*.

Schultze, C. 1969. The Role of Incentives Penalties and Rewards in Attaining Effective Policy, in Joint Economic Committee, *The Analysis and Evaluation of Public Expenditures: The PPB System*. Washington.

Wilde, J. A. June 1971. Grants-in-Aid: The Analytics of Design and Response. *National Tax Journal*.

COMMUNITY INCOME, INTERGOVERNMENTAL GRANTS, AND LOCAL SCHOOL DISTRICT FISCAL BEHAVIOR

Marvin B. Johnson

Introduction

Consumer demand theory often provides the basis for models of local government fiscal behavior. Like private consumers, local governments can be viewed as if they were maximizing a utility function subject to a budget constraint when they allocate resources between the public and private sectors. In the most commonly used variation of this approach, public goods and private goods are traded off, subject to the constraint that the sum of public and private local community spending cannot exceed community income plus grants-in-aid from other governments.

ACKNOWLEDGMENT. This paper was prepared for presentation at a meeting of the Committee on Urban Public Economics in New York on November 11–12, 1977. The comments and assistance of Peter Caulkins, Judith Collins, David Mack, Bernard Morzuch, Michael Wasylenko and Caryn Wirth, as well as the suggestions of the COUPE participants, especially those of William Fischel, Edward Gramlich, Robert Inman, Helen Ladd, and William Wheaton, are gratefully acknowledged. William Oakland made several very helpful suggestions. The author is responsible for all remaining errors and inadequacies. The research was supported by the College of Agricultural and Life Sciences in the University of Wisconsin-Madison, by Hatch Project 2316 and by a grant from the Wisconsin Graduate School. Marvin B. Johnson, University of Wisconsin-Madison.

This traditional constrained-maximization approach implies that disposable community income and intergovernmental grants have equivalent impacts on tax and spending levels. Not only is such an assumption awkward, but it also reduces the applicability of consumer behavior theory to governments (Bradford and Oates 1971b). Barro (1972) has proposed that the constrained-maximization model be recast so that its goal is to find the optimum combination of local public goods and locally imposed tax burden, subject to the constraint that public expenditures must not exceed taxes plus aid. If tax burden is defined as a function of both taxes and community income, then such a burden formulation allows aid and income to have different impacts on fiscal choices.

The problem is to untangle the relationships between community income, intergovernmental grants, and the fiscal behavior of local school districts. Specifically, do a dollar of lump sum school aid and a dollar of additional community income have the same effect on school expenditures and taxes? The roles of community income and intergovernmental grants in constrained-maximization models of local school district fiscal behavior are compared below. The implications of each model for a linear expenditure system (LES) based on a Stone-Geary specification of the utility function are drawn in pages 56 to 61. The appropriate form of the budget constraint for Wisconsin school districts in 1976–77 is developed in pages 61 to 69; section 5 (pages 69 to 75) is devoted to an empirical test of the hypothesis that community income and intergovernmental grants have equivalent impacts on fiscal behavior. A by-product of that test is a method for estimating models involving a kinked budget constraint.

Community Income and Grants in Constrained-Maximization Models

The conventional framework takes the community as the unit of analysis. Residents are viewed as choosing the combination of private goods (x) and public goods (e) which maximizes their well-being, subject to the constraint that community resources (R) are limited to the sum of private income (y) less federal taxes (t_f) and intergovernmental grants (g). The conventional model can be summarized mathematically:

Max $U(x, e)$
x, e subject to the constraint $x + e = R$
where $R = (y - t_f) + g = y_d + g$.

Grants and disposable (after federal tax) income (y_d) enter the resource constraint identically—unless (1) grants are perceived to depend on the level of x or e or, (2) g or y_d are arguments in the preference function. The constraint on the conventional model is that lump sum grants and disposable income have identical effects on community fiscal choices.

The possibility that grants depend on x or e can be incorporated in the conventional framework via an appropriate change in the resource constraint. Consider figure 1. In the absence of any grants, the community resource constraint is GH, where G is the disposable income of the community. A lump sum grant (k)—or an equivalent increase in disposable income—causes the resource constraint to shift out to IJ. If the community receives a matching grant based on public spending [$g_m = (1 - m)e$, where m is the fraction of e which must be raised locally], then the community resource constraint pivots out to IR.[1] The tangent of the resource constraint and the highest obtainable indifference curve (S) implies OW in public goods, OV in private goods and VG in taxes.[2] The effect of matching grants on recipient government spending behavior has been much analyzed using the conventional community utility-maximization approach (e.g., Scott 1952; Wilde 1968, 1971; Gramlich 1968).

The implicit assumption that lump sum grants and disposable income have identical effects on local government spending levels has been recognized by some researchers working with the traditional model. Wilde noted that "grants have been referred to as 'outside money,' which, having been raised by someone else, can be utilized in a different way from locally raised funds" (1968, p. 345). Gramlich and Galper explicitly allowed for the possibility that "lump sum transfers, which are already in the public treasury and therefore do not require the painful act of taxation, have a greater impact [than an equivalent increase in private income]" (1973, p. 23). They labelled this phenomenon the "flypaper theory of incidence"—money sticks where it hits—and found empirical support for it. Inman originally

---

1. The budget constraint in figure 1 assumes that the matching provisions are exogenous and known to the local government. These assumptions are not valid for all types of grants (Johnson, 1977a).

2. Expenditures are used as the proxy for goods throughout the paper. There is no adequate measure of education or government services. If prices of education services are constant—or if school decision makers actually use expenditures as their proxy for output—then this common but imperfect approach is acceptable.

Figure 1

CONVENTIONAL MODEL
LUMP SUM AND MATCHING GRANTS

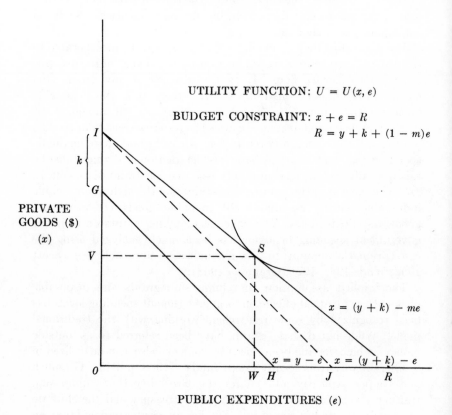

UTILITY FUNCTION: $U = U(x, e)$

BUDGET CONSTRAINT: $x + e = R$

$R = y + k + (1 - m)e$

PRIVATE
GOODS ($)
(x)

$x = (y + k) - me$

$x = y - e$ $x = (y + k) - e$

PUBLIC EXPENDITURES (e)

combined community income and grants into a single fiscal base variable, but found that "the results . . . make it clear that such a specification masks important differences in the effects of the two components" (p. 711). Bradford and Oates (1971a, 1971b) approached the problem by asking "whether there is some way the grantor might have distributed the grant funds directly to the individual members of the community such that precisely the same equilibrium state of the community would result" (as cited in Oates

1972, p. 108). Despite recognition of a bothersome implicit assumption, the community-based model remains the conventional approach. For example, Musgrave and Musgrave (1976) use it in their chapter on the theory of grants, although observing in a footnote that "the text argument implies that it makes no difference whether the money is given to the government or to the consumer directly" (p. 632).

Careful studies based on explicit community utility functional forms, such as those by Gramlich (1968 and 1969), Gramlich and Galper (1973), and Inman (1971), modify the conventional model to allow for flypaper effects. The adjustment invariably involves including income as an argument in the utility function. Such an adjustment is awkward in community-based models because it implies that *both* the budget constraint and the shape of the indifference curve depend on the level of disposable income. In figure 1, for example, both a lump sum grant and an increase in community income would be represented by a parallel outward shift of the resource constraint, but the latter also would involve a realignment of indifference curves.

The awkwardness disappears if the unit of analysis is shifted from the community to the local government decision-making unit. Such a shift is warranted because local governments are institutions, not perfect preference aggregators. Community preferences presumably are reflected in some fashion, but the fiscal decisions are made by a unit other than the community; that decision-making unit, not the community, should be the building block for the constrained maximization theory. The government unit can translate grants into private goods via tax reductions and income into public goods via tax increases, but what matters is where the money starts.

From the local government's perspective, the problem is to find the best combination of public services (e) and perceived tax burden (b), subject to the resource constraint that taxes must be raised to cover all outlays not paid for by grants. Tax burden, a negative good, depends on both the level of local taxes (t) and the community's ability to pay those taxes out of disposable income (y_a). Symbolically,

Max $U(e, b)$
e, t.
subject to the constraints
$e = t + g$
$b = b(t, y_a)$

If it is assumed that tax burden increases with tax levels and

decreases with disposable income, that the disutility of a given level
of local taxes declines with increasing income, and that the second
derivatives are all of the appropriate sign, a unique solution for e and t
is possible. The burden form of the model collapses to the conventional
form in the special case where the welfare of the local government
decision makers is decreased just as much by a decrease in community
income as by an equivalent increase in locally levied property taxes
(Barro 1972, pp. 15–17).

The burden form allows for the flypaper effect without the awkwardness of the conventional form. Consider figure 2. The budget
constraint in the absence of any grants is the 45-degree line emanating
from the origin. A lump sum grant of k causes a parallel downward
shift in the budget constraint (to the dotted line) by the amount of
the grant. Open-ended matching grants cause a downward pivot of the
budget constraint. In equilibrium (G), the government supports OH
in public expenditures by taxing OI and receiving grants of k and
$(1 - m)e$. The amount of private goods implicitly is the amount of
disposable income (y_d) less local taxes. An increase in y_d causes the
indifference map to shift, but does not affect the budget constraint.

Implication for a Linear Expenditure System

The contrasting roles of community income in the conventional
and tax burden models can be illustrated using a Stone-Geary
specification of the utility function which results in the well-known
linear expenditure system (LES). Other explicit forms for the
utility function have been used in the government spending-determi-
nants literature. Gramlich (1968; 1969) and Gramlich and Galper
(1973) have successfully employed an additive utility function with
quadratic terms in investigations of the impact of grants on state and
local government fiscal behavior. Henderson (1968) proposed a
simple multiplicative utility which has the convenient property that
maximization, subject to a budget constraint, yields a simple linear
behavioral equation. The major advantage of the Stone-Geary utility
function is that it is the only form which conforms to all the
properties of neoclassical microeconomic theory and also results in a
linear expenditure system (Stone 1954).

The LES has been widely used in the study of private consumption
patterns. Inman (1971) was the first to use the Stone-Geary utility
function and a LES to study public sector consumption patterns. His

Figure 2

TAX BURDEN MODEL

LUMP SUM AND MATCHING GRANTS

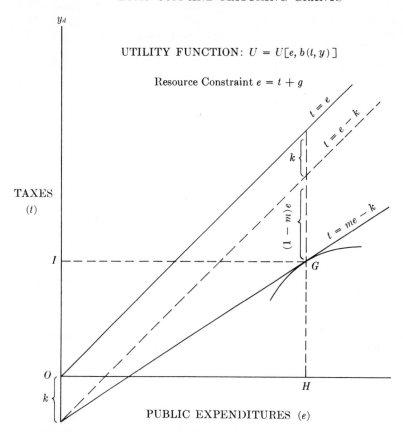

PUBLIC EXPENDITURES (*e*)

study identified the minimum acceptable levels of per capita spending by function for city governments, as well as the marginal budget share going to each "branch" or function for which the government accepted responsibility. Ehrenberg (1973) used a modified version of the Stone-Geary utility function in his study of the demand for state and

local government employees. Barro (1972) discussed the Stone-Geary
utility function as one possibility for specifying the demand relations
for local school districts, but he did not estimate any parameters.
A Stone-Geary specification was the basis for empirical work on the
fiscal behavior of Minnesota school districts in the second essay of my
dissertation (Johnson 1976).

The basic form of a Stone-Geary utility function is

$$U = \sum_{i=i}^{n} B_i \ln(q_i - \Pi_i)$$

where the B's and Π's are parameters with

$$0 < B_i < 1, \qquad 0 \leq \Pi_i, \qquad \sum_{i=i}^{n} B_1 = 1, \qquad \text{and}$$

$$0 < (q_i - \Pi_i).$$

The interpretation of the parameters in a Stone-Geary utility function
is straightforward. Given a level of income and a set of prices, the
consumer first purchases the minimum acceptable, or minimum
required, amount of each good (Π_i). Buying the minimum bundle of
all goods and services costs $\sum_i p_i \Pi_i$, the "subsistence" income. The
difference between total available income and the subsistence income
($y° - \sum_i p_i \Pi_i$) is the consumer's "supernumerary" income. These
funds are distributed among the goods (q_i) in proportion to the B
parameters; i.e., the B's are the marginal budget shares of each of the
goods. The Stone-Geary utility function constrains these shares to be
greater than zero (no inferior goods), less than one, and constant
(Goldberger 1967, pp. 47–48).

Before deriving and comparing the expenditure and tax equations
associated with a Stone-Geary utility function under the conventional
and the burden approaches, it is necessary to specify the two general
budget constraints for school districts. For the conventional community approach, school expenditures (e) less state aids (s) and
federal aids (f) plus private consumption (c) must equal disposable
income (y_d) (all in per student terms):

$$y_d = e - s - f + c.$$

State aids to schools, at least in Wisconsin, consist of a lump sum
component and a variable-term matching component. In the matching
component, local districts are expected to pay a "share" (m) of

operating expenditures, and the state pays the remaining share in general aids. The traditional budget constraint can be rewritten:

$$y = me - k + c,$$

where k is lump sum aids from all sources per student. Alternatively, since taxes per student (t) are equal to the difference between (y) and (c), the same budget constraint can be expressed without reference to (c) for use in the tax burden formulation:

$$t = me - k.$$

Combining the conventional approach and a Stone-Geary specification yields:

$$U = B_1 \ln (e - \Pi_2) + B_2 \ln (c - \Pi_2)$$

where B_1 = share of additional dollar going to educational spending;
$\quad\quad B_2$ = share of additional dollar going to private consumption;
$\quad\quad \Pi_1$ = minimum acceptable level of educational spending;
and $\quad \Pi_2$ = minimum acceptable level of private spending.

Maximizing U, subject to the appropriate budget constraint, yields two conditions:

$$\frac{B_1(c - \Pi_2)}{B_2(e - \Pi_1)} = m$$

and

$$y - c = e - k.$$

Solving for e and c in terms of exogenous variables yields:

$$e = B_2\Pi_1 + B_1 \left(\frac{v + k}{m}\right) - B_1\Pi_2 \left(\frac{1}{m}\right)$$

and

$$c = B_1\Pi_2 + B_2 (y + k) - B_2\Pi_1 (m).$$

If m is interpreted as the price of a dollar of e in terms of local taxes, then these equations are the standard linear expenditure system. Nothing in the conventional model indicates that community income should not be combined with lump sum grants.

The tax burden model specifies the local school district decision maker's utility level to be a strongly separable function of expenditures per student and tax burden. Tax burden, in turn, depends on the level of taxes and income per student. The easiest way to incorporate these changes in a Stone-Geary specification is to specify the maximum tax burden as a linear function of disposable income:

$$U = B_1 \ln (e - \Pi_1) + B_2 \ln (\Pi_2{}^* - t)$$

where

$$\Pi_2{}^* = \gamma_0 + \gamma_1 y_d = \text{maximum acceptable level of taxes.}$$

Maximizing subject to the relevant budget constraint again yields two conditions:

$$\frac{B_1 (\Pi_2{}^* - t)}{B_2 (e - \Pi_1)} = m$$

and

$$t = me = k,$$

but the resulting LES is

$$e = B_2\Pi_1 + B_1 \left(\frac{k}{m}\right) + B_1\gamma_1 \left(\frac{y}{m}\right) + B_1\gamma_0 \left(\frac{1}{m}\right)$$

and

$$t = B_1\gamma_0 + B_1\gamma_1(y) + B_2\Pi_1 m - B_2(k).$$

Consider the expenditure equations which result from the conventional and the tax burden approaches.[3] If γ_1 equals one, then the burden equation reduces to the equation implied by the conventional model. If γ_1 is not equal to one, then community income and lump sum grants have different impacts on government expenditures. A reasonable hypothesis is that γ_1 is less than one, or that the "fly-

---

3. Observe that the difference between what has been called the tax burden model and the conventional model is due strictly to the treatment of the income variable in the utility function and not to the specification of the budget constraint and the other "good" in terms of taxes. For example, Π_2 could be specified to be a linear function of income in the traditional model:

$$U = B_1 \ln (e - \Pi_1) + B_2 (c - \Pi_2{}^{**})$$

and

$$\Pi_2{}^{**} = \gamma_0{}^{**} + \gamma_1{}^{**} y.$$

The resulting expenditure function,

$$e = B_2\Pi_1 + B_1 \left(\frac{k}{m}\right) + B_1 (1 - \gamma_1{}^{**}) \left(\frac{y}{m}\right) - B_1\gamma_0{}^{**} \left(\frac{1}{m}\right)$$

reduces to the equation implied by the conventional approach if $\gamma_1{}^{**}$ equals zero. Thus, so long as the shape of the decision makers' indifference curves depends on community income, lump sum grants and community income will have different impacts on local government fiscal behavior.

paper theory of incidence" is correct.[4] Thus, the proposition to be tested empirically is whether γ_1 is less than one.

Budget Constraint for Wisconsin School Districts

The units of observation on which the empirical section of this paper is based are local Wisconsin school districts in 1976–77. Besides being readily available, school district data have several advantages over city data for a study of this type. One advantage is that the additive separability assumption required in the specification of a LES is more plausible for school districts than for cities because school districts have a single function. A second advantage of studying the local school districts in a single state is the availability of a large number of observations on independent governmental units operating within a common legal and fiscal framework, an important consideration, given that the estimators of the parameters of a LES system have desirable properties only asymptotically. The third advantage is that, in a state such as Wisconsin which distributes state aid via a variant of the district power equalizing (DPE) aid scheme, the effective budget constraint for all school districts can accurately be approximated by the general form $t = me - k$. Demonstrating the validity of this assertion requires a rather detailed examination of the Wisconsin state aid scheme and its implications for the budget constraints faced by local school districts.

The budget constraint for a local school district means that total spending per student (e) must be supported by taxes per student (t), state aids per student or federal aids per student. Deductible receipts per student (d), including federal aids and categorical state aids, and state special transitional aids per student (sst) can be viewed as lump sum grants.[5] General state aids (sg) depend on the level of educational

---

4. If γ_1 equals one, then the two utility functions also are identical if $\Pi_2 = y - \Pi_2{}^*$, or the maximum acceptable tax burden equals the difference between community income per person and the minimum acceptable level of private consumption per student.

5. Federal aids and state categorical aids are lump sum because the amount of aid does not depend directly on the amount spent by the school district. Some participants in the COUPE conference were uncomfortable with lumping the two kinds of aid together into a single lump sum grant variable, and others questioned whether the grants were truly lump sum in character. The paper retains the grouping and the lump sum classification because these grants are quite different from general school aids, are treated identically in the state aid formula, and are more lump sum than matching. More practically, data on each type of grant individually was not available.

spending in the local district. These general aids, explicitly designed to be the equalizing component of the aid package, are open-ended variable-term matching grants. There are three components of general state aid to local school districts in Wisconsin: primary aids (sgp), secondary aids (sgs), and general transitional aids (sgt). Thus, the budget constraint can be rewritten:

$$t = (e - d) - (sgp + sgs + sgt + sst).$$

Before considering the components of aid, it is necessary to clarify the meaning of expenditures per pupil. When working with Wisconsin school districts, e is most conveniently defined as the total operating budget per student of the school district plus up to $100 per pupil in annual capital outlays and principal and interest on long-term indebtedness.[6] This measure is convenient because general aids are based on the notion that the state will pay a certain percentage of a district's shared costs, with shared costs per pupil (cs) defined as total operating costs per pupil plus up to $100 per pupil in other outlays, less deductible receipts per pupil. Deductible receipts are excluded from shared costs to insure that general state aid is based only on local tax effort and not on other aids. As a result, local taxes are equal to the difference between shared costs and general aid, plus special transitional aid:

$$t = cs - (sg + sst).$$

To see how general aids are related to e, each component of general state aids must be examined. Consider primary aids first. Primary shared costs are all shared costs up to a ceiling, $1,545 per student in 1976–77. The local school district is responsible for a percentage of all primary costs (mp) equal to the ratio of the total amount of equalized property valuation in the district (v) and the valuation guaranteed by the state for all primary costs (vgp). The remaining share of primary shared costs ($1 - mp$) is covered by primary aids:

$$sgp = (1 - mp)(cs)$$

where $mp = \dfrac{v}{vgp}$

---

6. Inclusion of a modest amount of capital-related outlays per student in e drastically simplifies the exposition without changing anything of substance. Moreover, such a measure is consistent with the Wisconsin legislature's view of an appropriate proxy for educational spending.

and $sgp \geq 0$.

If a district spent less than \$1,545 per student in 1976–77 (and thus had no secondary costs to share) and also did not receive any type of transitional aids, then the effective budget constraint was simple:

$$t = (mp)(cs)$$

If a district spent more than \$1,545 per student, the state still shared these secondary costs, but required the local share of the additional costs to be much higher. The secondary local share (ms) is calculated as before, only the secondary guaranteed value is much lower than the primary guaranteed value:

$$ms = \frac{v}{vgs}$$

where $vgs < vgp$.

Secondary aids are paid only on costs in excess of \$1,545:

$$sgs = (1 - ms)(cs - \$1,545).$$

Primary aids, equal to the state's share of \$1,545 in primary costs, become a lump sum grant for districts incurring secondary costs:

$$sgp = (1 - mp)(\$1,545).$$

Assuming that no transitional aids are paid a district incurring secondary costs, the budget constraint can be written:

$$t = ms(cs) - (ms - mp)(\$1,545).$$

Wisconsin's basic primary and secondary aid system is summarized in figure 3. There is a kink in the effective budget constraint at \$1,545 per student in shared costs. Above that point, the marginal price of educational spending with respect to locally raised taxes increases from mp to ms, an increase of about 61 percent under the 1976–77 provisions. Although its pattern is similar for all school districts, the level of the budget constraint depends on equalized valuation per student. A district with low v receives more general aid and needs to raise less from local taxes to support any level of expenditures than does a high v district. There are both income and substitution effects inherent to the grant scheme which encourage low v districts to spend more on education. These income and

Figure 3

BASIC PRIMARY AND SECONDARY AIDS EFFECT
ON A TYPICAL WISCONSIN SCHOOL DISTRICT
BUDGET CONSTRAINT

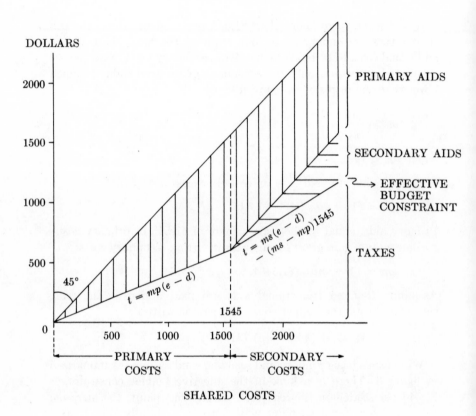

substitution effects operate on both sides of the kink, although the disincentives to higher spending by *v* rich districts are probably more important above the primary cost ceiling.

Figure 4 depicts how the Wisconsin system fulfills the district power-equalizing goal of assuring that an equal property tax rate is

Figure 4

REQUIRED TAX RATES VS. SHARED COSTS

WISCONSIN SCHOOL DISTRICTS

1976–77

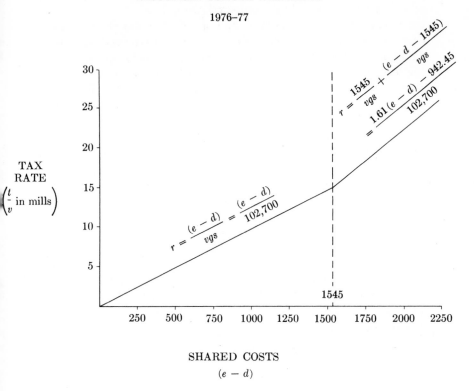

SHARED COSTS

$(e - d)$

required of all districts for any level of spending. The required local tax rate equals the shared costs divided by the *vgp* ($102,700 in 1976–77 for kindergarten through twelfth grade districts) for all primary costs. Districts incurring secondary costs must levy the maximum required primary rate plus a required secondary rate equal to secondary costs divided by the smaller secondary guaranteed valuation ($63,800 in 1976–77). Again, there is a kink at shared costs equal to $1,545, indicating that a dollar increase in shared costs necessitates a larger absolute increase in the local tax rate beyond the primary ceiling, but nearly all districts must tax their own property at an equal rate for equal expenditures per students.

Negative secondary aids occur under the Wisconsin system for all school districts that have property valuations in excess of the secondary guaranteed valuation and spend in excess of the primary cost ceiling. The budget constraint for such a district is illustrated in figure 5. The district receives positive primary aids for spending up to the primary cost ceiling, but these aids are offset by negative secondary aids (range 1). Above a certain level of spending, net aids are negative—or the district would owe the state money.

Negative aids are also implied by the Wisconsin—or any other *DPE*—school aid formula for all districts whose property valuation exceeds the level guaranteed by the state. Negative net aids were included as part of the 1973 school finance reform package in Wisconsin, but were declared in violation of the uniformity provision of the state constitution by the State Supreme Court in December, 1976. As a result of that decision, several very property-rich districts neither received nor paid general primary or secondary school aids.[7]

In 1976–77, property-rich and other school districts were eligible for both regular and special transitional aids. Regular transitional aids (*sgt*) were paid on the basis of any positive difference between total general aids received in base year 1972 (*B*) and the sum of primary and secondary general aids. In 1976–77, 60 percent of the difference was refunded. Thus,

$$sgt = \max\ [O,\ .6(B - sgp - sgs)]$$

Special transitional aids (*sst*) were paid to districts receiving general transitional aids that were adversely affected by the loss of taxable property due to the recent exemption of manufacturing machinery and equipment. These payments, over and above all types of general school aids, amounted to a little more than two million dollars. Most of these aids (85.5 percent) went to the urban districts in Madison and in Milwaukee County.

Five possible types of budget constraints for Wisconsin school districts in 1976–77 are summarized in table 1. These constraints all were derived from the basic budget identity that taxes equal expendi-

---

7. The impact of nonnegative aid constraints on fiscal equity among Wisconsin school districts has been analyzed by Johnson (1977b).

Figure 5

NEGATIVE SECONDARY AIDS

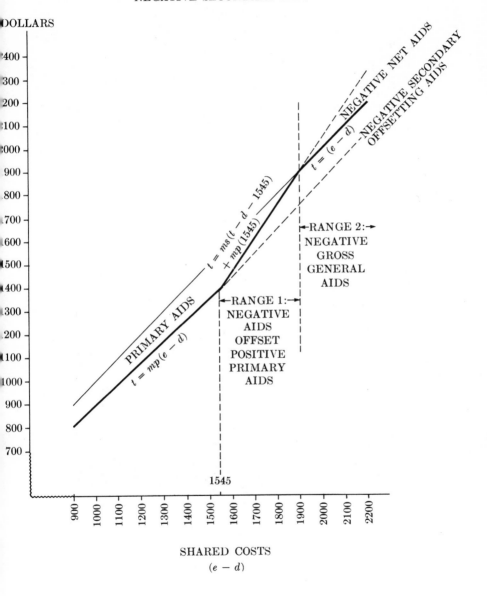

SHARED COSTS
$(e - d)$

Table 1

EFFECTIVE MARGINAL LOCAL "SHARES" OF EDUCATIONAL EXPENDITURES (m) AND EFFECTIVE LUMP SUM COMPONENTS OF PER STUDENT AIDS (k) WISCONSIN SCHOOL DISTRICTS 1976–77

	mp	Transitional Aid	Net General Aid	m	k
Primary Cost Districts	$mp < 1$	no	positive	mp	$(mp)(d) + sst$
Total Shared Costs $\leq$ $1,545 Per Student	$mp > 1$	yes	positive $(.6 + .4\,mp)$	$(.6 + .4\,mp)$	$(.6 + .4\,mp)(d) + .6B + sst$
Secondary Shared Costs	$mp \leq 1$	no	positive	ms	$(ms)(d) + (ms - mp)$ $(\$1,545) + ss$
Total Shared Cost > $1,545 Per Student	$mp \gtrless 1$	yes	positive $(.6 + .4\,ms)$	$(.6 + .4\,ms)$	$(.6 + .4\,ms)(d) + (618)$ $(ms - mp)\,.6B + sst$
	$mp \gtrless 1$	yes	zero	1	$d + sst$

mp = primary share = min $[1, v/\$102,700]$
ms = secondary share = $v/\$63,800$
d = deductible receipts per student
b = 1972 base aid per student
sst = state special transitional aid per student

General form of budget constraints:

$$t = me - k$$

tures less aids and from the above description of the various aid programs. In each case, local taxes per student equal some fraction (m) of shared costs less some constant (k).

Empirical Evidence

Because the effective budget constraint for all local school districts in Wisconsin can be approximated over the relevant range by $t = me - k$, an application of the tax burden model leads to the LES developed in section 3. As before, the tax burden model reduces to the traditional model if γ_1 equals one, and lump sum grants and community income have identical influences on school district fiscal behavior. To statistically test the null hypothesis that γ_1 equals one, assumptions must be made about the error structure in the LES system, proxies for y_d, m, k, and the other taste variable must be specified, the adjustments to the special problems associated with kinked budget constraints must be made, the unconstrained version of the system must be calculated and used. Each of these steps is taken in turn.

It is conventional to assume that the disturbances enter the functions of an LES additively; i.e.,

$$ e = B_2\Pi_1 + B_1\left(\frac{k}{m}\right) + B_1\gamma_1\left(\frac{y}{m}\right) + B_1\gamma_0\left(\frac{1}{m}\right) + u $$

and

$$ t = B_1\gamma_0 + B_1\gamma_1(y) + B_2\Pi_1(m) - B_2(k) + v $$

where u and v are disturbance terms. The budget constraint requires that the disturbance terms for each observation sum to zero (Pollack and Wales 1969). In this case, the budget constraint requires that v be the negative of u for each local school district. Taxes per student are a residual in the sense that they adjust passively to the independent disturbances in the educational expenditure function so as to satisfy the balanced budget constraint. Thus, it is necessary to estimate only one of the two equations in the system. Although either function would be appropriate, only the more common educational expenditure function is used here.

The units of observation are local Wisconsin school districts during

1976–77.[8] Educational expenditures per student (e) are measured by the total current operating budget plus up to $100 in nonoperating outlays per student. Community income per student (y) is net taxable income per student of the district's residents, where net taxable income is all taxable income less itemized and standard deductions. The income data is for 1974, the only prior year in which the Wisconsin Department of Revenue compiled such data by school district. The effective marginal "price" of educational spending in terms of locally raised taxes (m) is defined by table 1. The effective lump sum component of per student state aids (k) also is defined in table 1 or, equivalently, as the difference between total aids and the state's effective share of e. Component (k) is divided into two further components: "real" lump sum grants (k_r) comprised of deductable receipts and special transitional aids and "implicit" lump sum grants (k_i) attributable to the kink in the budget constraint.

Factors other than community income, lump sum grants, and the relative price of educational expenditures have been found to influence local school fiscal behavior (Denzau 1975). Two methods of explicitly recognizing influences other than price and income on spending behavior are common in cross-sectional studies of private consumption patterns. One is to subclassify the sample by that characteristic. The other is to "translate" the demand system by postulating that certain parameters are functions of the consumption unit's characteristics (Howe 1977). Both approaches were used here.

The population of all school districts in the state was divided into three classes according to type of service provided: K-12, K-8, or Union High School. Each type receives aid under a different formula. Ideally, parameter estimates would have been generated for each type of district and tests run to determine if the different types of districts behave differently. Unfortunately, unavailability of data and small sample sizes for the 11 Union High School districts and 53 K-8 districts prohibited any such empirical comparisons. Thus, the sample was limited to 370 districts operating grades K-12. The only K-12 districts excluded from the sample were the Menominee Indian District and the Norris Foundation, a special education district.[9]

8. All data are from the Wisconsin Department of Public Instruction and the Wisconsin Legislative Council Staff.

9. The 370 school districts included in the sample account for about 97 percent of the districts that operate high schools, 96 percent of the school enrollment, 95 percent of the equalized value, 97 percent of total aids, and 95 percent of local school property taxes in the state.

The minimum acceptable level of educational spending parameter (Π_1) is specified to be a linear function of other characteristics of the school district or its population.[10] Specifically, it is postulated that

$$\Pi_1 = a_0 + \sum_{i=i}^{n} a_i X_i ,$$

where the X_i are proxies for exogenous "taste" variables which have been found to influence a local school district's fiscal behavior. Five such variables were included: a dummy variable indicating fiscal dependence on a municipality (X_5), size proxied by resident enrollment (X_6), property valuation per student (X_7),[11] percent of resident students attending local public schools (X_8) and percent of students from nonminority backgrounds (X_9).

The kinked budget constraint inherent to the Wisconsin system of school aids poses two unique problems. First, the lump sum grant (k) described in the previous sector is the sum of a "real" lump sum grant (k_r) and an implicit lump sum grant (k_i). Consider figure 6. Real lump sum grants consist of special state transition aids (sst) and

---

10. Note that it is also possible to make the marginal budget share parameter (B_1) a linear function of the X characteristics. Because LES constrains the B's to sum to one, this "translation" unduly complicates the procedure. Thus it is assumed here that marginal budget shares are constant across districts, but that the minimum acceptable level of per student educational spending varies and depends on $X_5 \ldots X_9$.

11. Including valuation per student as a "taste" variable is based on the notion that property taxes support schools and that property valuation per student is one proxy for ability to pay school taxes. There are at least three objections to including valuation per student in the analysis: (1) it is highly collinear with other independent variables, notably the inverse of the marginal local share; (2) it is simultaneously determined (via capitalization relocation) with fiscal policies; and (3) it neglects the price effect inherent in the composition of the local property tax base (Ladd 1975). Although each of these objections has some merit, the valuation per student variable remains in the analysis. Valuations per student are correlated with the inverse of m $(r = .-62)$, but I maintain that valuation per student is a relevant variable. Omission of valuation per student causes the price of other goods (the inverse of m) to "pick-up" the influence of valuation on expenditures—and have a statistically significant wrong (negative) sign. Expenditures and property valuation per student may very well be simultaneously determined, but the data on the determinants of property valuation (especially net migration) required for a meaningful estimate of a simultaneous-equation system are not available for Wisconsin school districts. The unavailability of data also precludes the inclusion of a tax base composition variable in the analysis, although the "export effect" is much smaller, or even nonexistent, under DPE schemes (Johnson and Collins, 1978).

Figure 6

REAL AND IMPLICIT LUMP SUM GRANTS
WISCONSIN SCHOOL DISTRICTS
1976–77

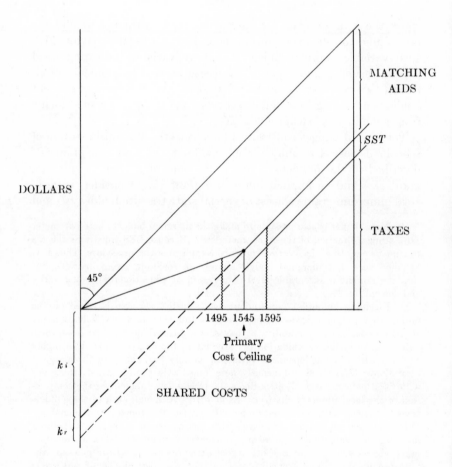

deductible receipts (not shown) which reduce shared costs. The "implicit" component of effective lump sum grants in the budget constraint is only implied by the matching provision. Equalizing aid for secondary cost districts is the sum of a lump sum amount for primary costs incurred (k_i) and a possibly negative amount based on the level of secondary costs. It seems unreasonable to constrain real and implicit lump sum grants to have the same impact on educational spending; the empirical model thus is modified to include both k_r and k_i as independent variables to allow for different impacts.

The second problem is closely related to the first. The spending level of many school districts places them near the kink in the budget constraint. As a district goes from just below to just above the kink, both its marginal share and its implicit lump sum grant increase sharply. Thus m and k_i are very sensitive to whether a district is above or below the primary cost ceiling. Yet many of these districts probably intend to spend about at the kink and are not much affected if they end up a little high or low. It seems plausible that eliminating the district's spending in the range immediately surrounding the kink (between the wavy lines in figure 6) might lead to better estimates.

The basic unconstrained estimating equation, including the new Π_1 specification and the two components of k, takes the form

$$e = \phi_0 + \phi_1 \frac{k_r}{m} + Q_2 \left(\frac{k_i}{m}\right) + \phi_3 \left(\frac{y}{m}\right) + \phi_4 \left(\frac{1}{m}\right)$$

$$+ \sum_{i=5}^{9} \phi_i X_i + u,$$

where the disturbance term is assumed to conform to the classical assumptions. From this equation and the restriction that the sum of the marginal shared parameters (B's) is one, a unique solution for each of the restricted parameters in terms of the unrestricted coefficients can be obtained. The equation is exactly identified because, unlike most cross-sectional consumption studies, the relative "price" of one good, educational spending per student, varies across observations. The parameter in question here, γ_1, is equal to ϕ_3 divided by ϕ_1, and is equal to one if ϕ_3 equals ϕ_1.

The ordinary least squares (OLS) estimates of the unrestricted coefficients for the "all districts" and the "gap at kink" cases are summarized in table 2. These results conform to the usual findings in

Table 2

UNCONSTRAINED (LES) REGRESSION COEFFICIENT
ESTIMATES FOR WISCONSIN K-12 SCHOOL DISTRICTS
1976–77

		All Districts	*Gap-at-Kink*
X_0:	constant	766.16	754.83
X_1:	$K_r \div m$ = real lump sum aids per student corrected for local share	1.61 (8.20)**	1.61 (7.13)**
X_2:	$K_i \div m$ = lump sum aids implicit in equalizing grant corrected for local share	.38 (9.37)**	.52 (10.74)**
X_3:	$y \div m$ = community income per student corrected for local share	.0058 (2.51)**	.0046 (1.79)*
X_4:	$1 \div m$ = inverse of local share of educational expenditures	6.53 (.28)	27.95 (1.09)
X_5:	a dummy variable = 1 if district is fiscally dependent	−18.87 (.81)	−22.32 (.83)
X_6:	size measured by resident enrollment (100's)	.16 (1.30)	.12 (.92)
X_7:	property valuation per student ($1,000)	1.89 (4.66)**	2.46 (5.50)**
X_8:	percent of resident students enrolled in local public schools	2.37 (3.53)**	1.82 (2.17)**
X_9:	percent of student from nonminority backgrounds	1.64 (1.61)	1.62 (1.53)
R^2:		.578	.662
n:		370	280
$\bar{R}^2$:		.568	.650

* Significantly greater than zero at .05 level.
** Significantly greater than zero at .01 level.
Absolute value to t statistics are in parenthesis.

the school expenditure literature. Per student expenditures are positively related to both real and implicit lump sum grants per student, community income per student, school district size, valuation per pupil, percent of resident students attending local schools, and percent of students who are from nonminority backgrounds and are negatively related to fiscal dependence on a municipality. Coefficients for community income, property valuation, public enrollment, and the two grants are significantly greater than zero at .05 level or better.

The corresponding estimates of the γ_1 parameter, generated from the unrestricted coefficients on X_1 and X_3 via the solution noted above, are .0036 (all districts case) and .0028 (gap-at-kink case). It is clear that γ_1 is less than one and that a dollar of lump sum grants per student has a much larger impact on educational spending than does a dollar of community income per student.[12] For completeness, however, a statistical test of that finding is presented.

The estimator for γ_1, like all estimators that are nonlinear functions of unconstrained coefficients, is consistent but not unbiased (Kmenta 1971, p. 166). Thus, the estimators of ϕ_3 and ϕ_1 are unbiased, but the γ_1 estimator based on them is not. However, the bias of the γ_1 estimator is mitigated by the relatively large sample sizes. The large-sample variance for the γ_1 estimator can be approximated by a formula involving the sample variances and covariances of the unrestricted estimators (Kmenta, p. 444). The standard errors for γ_1, based on the above formula, are about .0000020 and .0000025. The resulting absolute values of the t statistics are very large, and the null hypothesis that γ_1 equals 1 must be rejected.[13] The flypaper theory is supported.

Summary

The simple notion that community income and intergovernmental grants have different impacts on local government fiscal behavior was the rather modest core of this paper. Empirical support for that notion, based on the application of a Stone-Geary utility function to

---

12. At the COUPE conference, Robert Inman observed that this very small income effect modestly overstates the effect of income on spending because it neglects the price distortion inherent in a progressive federal income tax featuring local tax deductibility.

13. The γ_i based on k_j rather than k_r is also statistically insignificant.

the budget problem faced by local school districts in Wisconsin during 1976–77, was offered. The results imply that community income and intergovernmental grants must enter constrained maximization models of government spending decisions differently. One convenient way to accomplish this is to postulate that income influences the decision maker's taste for public services. The traditional model of public versus private good can be modified to include community income as a taste variable, but such a modification leads to the confusion of having both the budget constraint and the preference pattern influenced by community income. By taking the local government, rather than the community, as the unit of observation, the tax burden approach has the additional advantage of explicitly recognizing that governments are not perfect preference aggregators.

REFERENCES

Barro, S. M. 1972. *Theoretical Models of School District Expenditure Determination and the Impact of Grants-in-Aid.* Santa Monica: Rand Corporation Monograph R-867-FF.

Bradford, David F., and Oates, Wallace E. 1971a. Towards a Predictive Theory of Intergovernmental Grants. *American Economic Review* 61: 440–48.

Bradford, David F., and Oates, Wallace E. 1971b. An Analysis of Revenue Sharing. *Quarterly Journal of Economics* 85: 416–39.

Denzau, Arthur. 1975. An Empirical Survey of Studies on Public School Financing. *National Tax Journal* 18: 241–49.

Ehrenberg, Ronald G. 1973. The Demand for State and Local Government Employees. *The American Economic Review* 63: 366–79.

Fredland, John Eric. 1974. Determinants of State and Local Expenditures: An Annotated Bibliography. Washington, D.C.: An Urban Institute Contract Report.

Goldberger, Arthur S. 1967. *Functional Form and Utility: A Review of Consumer Demand Theory.* Madison, Wisconsin: Systems Formulation, Methodology and Policy Workshop Paper.

Gramlich, Edward M. 1968. Alternative Federal Policies for Stimulating State and Local Expenditures. *National Tax Journal* 21: 119–29.

———. 1969. State and Local Governments and Their Budget Constraint. *International Economic Review* 10: 163–82.

Gramlich, Edward M., and Galper, Harvey. 1973. State and Local Fiscal Behavior and Federal Grant Policy. *Brookings Papers on Economic Activity* 1: 15–65.

Henderson, James. 1968. Local Government Expenditures: A Social Welfare Analysis. *Review of Economics and Statistics* 50: 156–63.

Howe, Howard. Feb. 1977. Cross-Section Application of Linear Expenditure

Systems: Responses to Sociodemographic Effects. *American Journal of Agricultural Economics*, pp. 141–48.

Inman, Robert P. 1971. Toward an Econometric Model of Local Budgeting. *National Tax Association: Proceedings of the Sixty-Second Annual Conference on Taxation*, pp. 699–719.

Johnson, Marvin B. 1976. Two Essays on the Modelling of State and Local Government Fiscal Behavior. Ph.D. Dissertation, Syracuse University.

—————. 1977a. Recognizing the Competitive Nature of General Revenue Sharing Grants. *Southern Economic Journal* 44: 143–47.

—————. Dec. 1977b. Nonnegative Aid Constraints and Fiscal Equity Among Local School Districts. Presented at Allied Social Science Association Annual Meeting.

Johnson, Marvin B., and Collins, Judith N. July 1978. Equalizing Matching Grants and the Allocative and Distributive Objectives of Public School Financing: Comment. *National Tax Journal*.

Kmenta, Jan. 1971. *Elements of Econometrics*. New York: MacMillan.

Ladd, Helen. 1975. Local Education Expenditures, Fiscal Capacity and the Composition of the Property Tax Base. *National Tax Journal* 28: 145–58.

Musgrave, Richard A., and Musgrave, Peggy B. 1976. *Public Finance in Theory and Practice* 2d ed. New York: McGraw Hill.

Oates, Wallace E. 1972. *Fiscal Federalism*. New York: Harcourt Brace Jovanovich.

Pollack, Robert A., and Wales, Terence J. 1969. Estimation of the Linear Expenditure System. *Econometrica* 37: 611–28.

Scott, A. D. 1952. The Evaluation of Federal Grants. *Economica* 19: 377–94.

Stone, J. R. N. 1954. Linear Expenditure Systems and Demand Analysis: An Application to the Pattern of British Demand. *Economic Journal* 64: 511–27.

Wilde, James A. 1968. The Expenditure Effects of Grant-in-Aid Programs. *National Tax Journal* 21: 340–48.

—————. 1971. Grants-in-Aid: The Analytics of Design and Response. *National Tax Journal* 24: 143–55.

Wisconsin Department of Public Instruction. 1977a. Basic Facts About Wisconsin's Elementary and Secondary Schools, 1967–77 School Year. Bulletin no. 7353. Madison.

—————. 1977b. General School Aid Budget Estimates for 1976–1977. Madison.

Wisconsin Department of Public Instruction. 1977c. *Planning for Better Education in Wisconsin: A Guide for Agency School Committees, 1976–77 Data Supplement*. Bulletin no. 7446. Madison.

Wisconsin Legislative Council Staff. Ranking of School Districts 1975–76 on Equalized Valuation Per Member, Income Per Member, Tax Rate, Cost Per Member and Membership. Information Memorandum 76-28.

DISCUSSION OF MARVIN B. JOHNSON, "COMMUNITY INCOME, INTERGOVERNMENTAL GRANTS, AND LOCAL SCHOOL DISTRICT FISCAL BEHAVIOR"

William A. Fischel, Discussant

This paper may be viewed as attempting to show two things. The more successful demonstration is that there does appear to be a "flypaper" effect from grants-in-aid in yet another sample of local governments. This is an important result, as there is widely varying evidence on whether additional community resources in the form of private income or public grants have different effects on local expenditures. Professor Johnson's careful study surely moves the balance of this evidence towards the opinion that nominally unrestricted grants-in-aid have a substantially greater effect on local spending than similar increments to private income.

The second objective is to reformulate a model of local government decision making to account for the flypaper effect. The tax burden model developed by Johnson can be seen as serving two purposes. One is simply to provide a context in which to interpret the difference between private and public budget constraints. This allows for a more convenient econometric interpretation of the two sources of "income," since private income can now be viewed as a taste variable by local officials. The second purpose, which necessarily follows from

NOTE. I have benefited from written comments on Prof. Johnson's paper by Paul Courant, Robert Inman, Helen Ladd, and William Wheaton, as well as from oral remarks I recorded during the presentation. The present discussion includes much of my own interpretation, so the aforementioned individuals cannot be held responsible for the errors which may appear.

the first, is to ground the issue in some plausible maximizing hypotheses about consumer theory. It is this second purpose which disturbed several conference participants.

What is most bothersome about the tax burden model is the seemingly ad hoc nature of the utility function for the local government managers. They like spending, they don't like to raise taxes, and the trade-offs they make are determined by the characteristics of their constitutents, especially their income. This is a bit like saying that honeybees coordinate their activities by instinct. It just puts the problem off one more step. Local officials surely are not autonomous; they would not be concerned by taxes in that case. They are clearly not perfect preference aggregators, either; otherwise, our conventional voting models would be satisfactory. The degree of autonomy (or responsiveness to voters) of the managers is presumably reflected in their indifference curves. But that is just calling it instinct. Before we accept models like this, we have to specify the apparently complex political relationships which exist among voters, local officials, grant administrators, and granting government legislators. Once these are specified, it *may* be useful to incorporate them as different functional forms for a utility function for a local government official. The present paper shows that this approach can account for some phenomena in which we are interested, but it does not convince us that we have gained any insights into economic behavior.

Besides the preceding theoretical issue, there are some empirical questions which ought to be raised. The first is that much of the school aid seems to be narrowly defined and may come from a variety of sources. This might tend to reduce its fungibility, so that it is not quite fair to compare this to very general types of grants. We would expect to see large expenditure effects even in the conventional model in this case.

A second possible improvement in the empirical work would be to account for the effect of federal tax deductions on local property taxes. Higher local expenditures cost less to rich communities than to others, and the already small income effects which Johnson's results indicate may be overstated.

Including the entire local property tax base as a community wealth variable is not satisfactory for several reasons. The chief one is that there may be substantial differences in the fraction of commercial and industrial property between different districts. Since this fraction may be a choice variable (via municipal zoning decisions), an important element of simultaneity may be introduced, creating bias in estimating the expenditure equations.

A final point deals with how decision makers know what the community budget constraints are. It was pointed out that a large number of communities in the sample seem to lie very close to the "kink" in the budget constraint. It may be that they actually believe they are on it, and hence their constraint is indeterminant. It would be interesting to know what the results would be if these districts were removed from the sample.

The general consensus among the conference participants was that this paper is an interesting and very useful contribution to the literature on grants in the federal economy. There was much admiration of Professor Johnson's ability to produce such a paper on rather short notice. The paper is useful both as an addition to our empirical knowledge of intergovernmental grants and as a reminder that we need to learn more about the complex institutional arrangements of the grants economy. We know that simple explanations are not satisfactory. The agenda for future research should include some comparative studies of various institutions in order to learn more about the grant process itself.

AN ECONOMIC MODEL OF THE DISTRIBUTION OF PROJECT GRANTS

Howard A. Chernick

This paper studies the economic consequences of an administrative allocation system for distributing grants-in-aid in a federalist system. In so doing, a link is made between topics in two separate areas—the economic theory of bureaucratic behavior, and the study of fiscal federalism. The rationale for this link is that as the form of inter-governmental financing shifts towards grants-in-aid which allow a greater potential for discretionary behavior on the part of the bureaus charged with distributing that aid, the incentives and behavioral characteristics of such agencies become important in explaining the allocational outcomes of a federal system.

[Dr. Chernick is in the Office of Income Security of the Department of Health, Education and Welfare.]

NOTE. This paper is based on the author's doctoral dissertation, "The Economics of Bureaucratic Behavior: An Application to the Allocation of Federal Project Grants," University of Pennsylvania, 1976. An earlier version of this paper was presented at the August 1975 meetings of the World Econometric Society in Toronto. Support for the research was provided by the University of Pennsylvania, the Fels Center of Government, and by Abt Associates, Inc. The author would like to thank his thesis advisors, Robert Inman and Julius Margolis, for helpful comments and advice. Thanks are also due to Helen Ladd for her perceptive comments on the specification of the price discrimination model and to Andrew Reschowsky. The clarity of this paper's exposition was improved by comments from Daniel Weinberg and Andrew Reschovsky.

The type of grant-in-aid studied in this paper is the project grant. By *project grant* I refer to subventions which are distributed on a project-by-project basis. Under this form of grant-in-aid, no particular eligible unit is automatically entitled to a share. Communities must specifically apply for aid, generally by submitting a detailed written application. Distribution of aid is determined by administrative fiat.

In the 1960s the project grant became the dominant form of assistance in the United States. Of the 370 grant-in-aid authorizations as of January 1, 1967, 280 were project grants. One hundred of these 280 were enacted in the three-year period 1964–66.[1] The number of grants was reduced somewhat in the 1970s under the impetus of revenue-sharing and the "new federalism." However, the project grant continues to be an important means of allocating intergovern-mental aid, and may again grow in importance as new issues come onto the agenda of fiscal federalism.

There were two reasons for an increase in reliance on the project grant. For one, it provided a politically legitimate means of targeting aid to needy or deserving recipients, without the necessity of funding all potentially eligible units. By use of project grants, the federal government was able to bypass the states, considered to be un-sympathethic and relatively unresponsive to the problems and needs of the large cities, and award aid directly to the cities.

Schultze (1974) has pointed out a second reason, relating to the desired degree of federal control over local behavior. Many of the grants which developed in the 1960s provided funding for goods and services which were previously unproduced by localities. Rather than open-ended price subsidies, the relevant paradigm was essentially one of centrally determined goods, with local communities acting as contractors or subcontractors in production. Since programs reflected federal preferences, funding was accompanied by detailed federal specification of the exact nature of the good or service to be produced. Such a contractual model called for a more efficacious means of control than was available under automatic entitlement grants. The project grant model, by forcing communities to compete for limited funds via detailed written application, provided an ostensibly superior ex ante control mechanism, and by the threat of nonrenewal of funds, a superior set of ex post performance sanctions.

Economic literature with insight into bureaucratic behavior has

---

1. ACIR (1967).

been relatively sparse. Two strands exist. The first, exemplified by the work of Downs and Tullock, examines the informational character- istics of bureaus, and the incentives facing individual bureaucrats.[2] These studies stress the role that loss of control across hierarchical levels plays in leading to bureau ossification and individual behavior inconsistent with the higher objectives of the agency.

A more recent line of inquiry develops a theory of resource alloca- tion conditioned by bureaucratic supply.[3] Attempts are made to determine the equilibrium level of output under bureaucratic supply, usually assuming that the objective function of the chief bureaucrat is to maximize the bureau's budget. These studies posit a bilateral bargaining model; the relevant actors are the legislative committee and the bureau. The level and type of output are determined by the demand curve of the Congress, and the costs of monitoring the bureau. A major hypothesis advanced is that monopoly bureaus are able to exploit the bilateral bargaining relationship, and increase output and expenditures to a greater than optimal level.

This paper develops a theory of bureaucratic behavior in the distribution of discretionary project grants-in-aid. The analysis builds on the work of Niskanen in adopting an explicit utility maximization framework to characterize the behavior of the bureau- cratic grantor. However, because the focus is on the interaction between the grant recipient and the bureaucrat, the project grant budget is assumed to be fixed. The basic argument is that the bureau behaves as a price discriminator in the quasi-market in federal aid which emerges from a project grant system. In this market, different matching rates act as prices in allocating resources.

Much of the previous empirical research on fiscal federalism has been devoted to the question of the expenditure-inducement effects of various types of grants-in-aid.[4] The typical study regresses local expenditures on the level of grants-in-aid, and a vector of exogenous spending determinants. The more sophisticated econometric work attempts to distinguish the price and income effects of grants-in-aid.[5] In these studies, levels of aid and matching rates are exogenously determined.

2. Anthony Downs (1967); Gordon Tullock, (1965).

3. See William Niskanen (1971) and Breton and Wintrobe (1975).

4. Two summaries of this literature are provided by Gramlich (1969) and Gramlich (1977).

5. See Inman (1971), and Gramlich and Galper (1973).

In contrast, this paper develops a model which endogenizes the level of aid received by different communities.[6] As implied by a theory of price discrimination, the dollar amount of aid is shown to depend on the local willingness to pay for federal aid, where willingness to pay is defined in terms of the rate at which the locality is willing to match federal grants of different dollar amounts. The aid model is tested empirically, and the results are found to be consistent with price discrimination behavior on the part of the grantor. In showing the level of aid to be dependent on local behavioral parameters, the results suggest that models of the stimulative effect of intergovernmental aid which do not incorporate this endogeneity may be misspecified.

The model also implies that the level of project aid should depend on differences in the grantor's marginal valuation of output in different communities. These marginal valuation functions are assumed to depend on specific community characteristics. The empirical test of this specification provides insight into two potentially important factors in the distribution of project grants-in-aid: political power and fiscal equalization.

The paper is organized as follows. Section 1 develops the model of bureaucratic behavior in the distribution of project aid. In section 2, an empirical test of the grant award model is presented, using data from the Basic Water and Sewer grant of the Department of Housing and Urban Development. A concluding section summarizes the major results.

A Model of Bureaucratic Behavior

The project grant manager's behavior is characterized by the maximization of a well-behaved utility function

$$U(Q^1 \ldots Q^n) , \tag{1}$$

the arguments of which are the potential outputs of grants in the n communities that apply for aid.[7] The rationale for making grantor utility a function of output in the applicant communities is that the

---

6. A model which explains variations in matching rates across communities is discussed in Chernick (1978).

7. The grant manager is that position or hierarchical level within the agency with direct responsibility for screening applicants and awarding aid.

creation of a set of readily identifiable outputs provides the most direct evidence that the program is achieving its goals. Inability to produce such outputs constitutes a prima facie case for the program's lack of merit, and is most likely to lead to contraction of funding or outright program rescission.[8]

The particular output measure adopted by the grantor depends on the degree of uncertainty in the production function for the aided good or service. The greater this uncertainty is, the greater the extent to which the grantor adopts intermediate rather than final measures of output, or uses inputs as criteria for project awards. The utility function approach implies a conceptual distinction between the gross physical benefits of the project and the valuation of the benefits. Utility weights are determined by a number of factors, including program intent as defined legislatively, the overall goals of the administering agency, and the idiosyncratic characteristics of program managers. These weights are revealed through observed patterns of project choice. Inconsistencies in bureaucratic decision making—i.e., choices which are in conflict with the weightings—are measured by the dispersion of the distribution decisions about these mean patterns.[9]

The grant manager maximizes (1) by distributing dollar amounts of aid G_i to a subset ($i = 1 \ldots, n_1$) of the n applicants. The utility function is assumed to have positive first partial derivatives ($U_i > 0$). Since output Q is a nondecreasing function of dollar inputs, the implication of this "non-satiation" assumption is that the grantor will always allocate the entire appropriation.

Grant administrators are subject to political pressures towards uniformity in the distribution of aid.[10] These pressures are translated into postulated cardinal restrictions on the second and cross partial derivatives of (1), namely $U_{ii} < 0$, and $U_{ij} \geq 0$.[11] The first describes a "spread-around" effect, saying that the marginal utility of increasing the amount of output (and hence aid) is a diminishing function of output in that community. The second, which I call the "me-too"

---

8. Program continuation is consistent with the bureaucratic budget maximization objective postulated by Niskanen (1971).

9. See McFadden (1975).

10. Even for discretionary project grants, a set of formally announced minimums constrains the geographic distribution of aid.

11. These restrictions are stronger than those ordinarily imposed on utility functions. While not strictly necessary, they represent a set of behavioral assumptions which may be empirically tested.

effect, is a complementarity assumption. If the grantor gives more aid to one community, the marginal utility of additional aid to all other communities is nondecreasing.

The utility function (1) is maximized subject to a program budget constraint given by

$$P_1 Q^1 + \ldots + P_n Q^n \leq Z, \tag{2}$$

where Z is the total appropriation for the program. The vector of prices (P) represents the net cost to the federal agency per unit of output for each applicant. Price to the grantor is related to output by an inverse supply function of the form

$$P_i = P_i(Q^i) = [1 - m_i(Q^i)] \cdot C_i(Q^i), \qquad i = 1 \ldots n. \tag{3}$$

For a given level of output, average federal cost depends on the average cost function $C(Q)$ and the local sharing function $m(Q)$. The latter, which is the inverse of the local supply or offer curve, gives the maximum local share or match which will be offered by a community for a grant to produce Q units of output. It is assumed that $m'(Q) \leq 0$. To increase Q, the grantor must not decrease his own share.[12]

Figures 1 through 3 illustrate the case of a U-shaped average cost curve $[C(Q)]$ and a local sharing function $[m(Q)]$ which is monotonically decreasing. The effect of the matching grant for Q is to rotate the local budget constraint towards Q. Figure 1 shows the local offer curve for Q for successively greater rates of federal matching. In figure 2 the federal inducement cost $[P(Q)]$ is shown. The largest output of Q which can be induced by a matching grant is Q_{max}. To induce output greater than this level, the grantor must bear the entire cost of the output. Conversely, the local matching rate $[m(Q)$ in fig. 3] declines monotonically from Q_0, the zero grant level of output, until it reaches zero at output Q_{max}. For the case illustrated, efficiency considerations will dictate a certain minimum project size. Although there is no reason to expect the minimum cost scale of project to be attained, such a cost curve will usually be sufficient to ensure that not all projects can be funded.

The award of aid may be viewed as a two-stage process. In the first stage the grantor determines which communities will receive grants,

---

12. This restriction is equivalent to the assumption of a demand curve for the aided output which is nonincreasing.

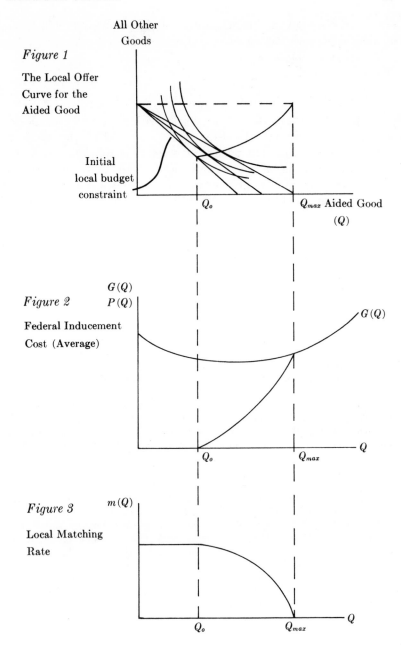

Figure 1

The Local Offer Curve for the Aided Good

All Other Goods

Initial local budget constraint

Q_o Q_{max} Aided Good
(Q)

Figure 2

Federal Inducement Cost (Average)

$G(Q)$
$P(Q)$

$G(Q)$

Q_o Q_{max} Q

Figure 3

Local Matching Rate

$m(Q)$

Q_o Q_{max} Q

while in the second the exact quantity of aid and the matching rate for that aid are negotiated with each individual community.[13]

Maximizing (1) with respect to Q^i, subject to (2), gives the first-order conditions

$$U_i/(p_i + p_i'Q^i) = -\lambda, \qquad (i = 1 \ldots n) \qquad (4)$$

where p_i' is the derivative of federal price with respect to a change in quantity in community i. The expression $(p_i + p_i'Q^i)$ is the marginal cost to the grantor of inducing an extra unit of output in community i.[14] Its value depends on the average price (p_i) and on the derivatives of $m(Q)$ and $c(Q)$.[15] If the grantor were utility neutral, i.e., indifferent between outputs in different communities, then (4) would reduce to

$$p_i + p_i' \cdot Q^i = -1/\lambda, \qquad i = 1 \ldots n \qquad (4a)$$

giving the decision rule that communities for which the marginal inducement cost exceeds $-1/\lambda$ will not be funded.[16] If (4a) were in fact the operant decision rule, then the award of aid would tend to favor more efficient communities [for which $C(Q)$ is lower] and

---

13. With a fixed and known appropriation, there is a determinate relationship between the dollar amount of the grant award and the number of communities which can be funded. However, the criteria which are used to decide which projects to fund may be different from those used to determine the level of funding for selected projects. The two-stage model is designed to test for such differences.

14. This measure of marginal cost reflects the assumption that the opportunity cost of additional output in one community is the foregone output in all other communities. Because of the bureaucratic insularity from other programs, the opportunity cost to the *grantor* of an extra dollar of *local* expenditures is zero.

15. As pointed out by Ladd in the discussion that follows this paper, an important assumption in this model is that the marginal inducement cost may differ across communities. A similar assumption is made by McGuire and Garn (1969) in their analysis of cost sharing and grants-in-aid.

16. Condition (4a) is equivalent to equation (3) in McGuire and Garn's (1969) analysis of cost sharing and grants-in-aid. These authors argue that the appropriate objective function should be to maximize the sum of the utilities of grant recipients, where each recipient's utility is a function of the level of the nonaided good G_N and the aided good Q. The first-order conditions for their model state that grants should be allocated so as to equate the marginal utility to each community of an extra dollar of federal aid. I argue that such an objective function is inappropriate as a positive behavioral model of the award of aid. Under the bureaucratic model, grant managers maximize their own utility, rather than that of the recipients of aid.

communities which offer to bear a higher proportion of project cost. *If wealthier communities are more efficient, or have a more price inelastic offer curve, then the equity implications of output maximization are clearly adverse.*

However, the assumption that federal grantors maximize utility, rather than output, implies that a community which is unwilling or unable to match federal expenditures at the requisite rate, i.e., for which $1/(p_i + p_i' \cdot Q^i) < -\lambda$, may still be awarded a grant because

$$U_i(p_i + p_i' \cdot Q^i) \geqq -\lambda.$$

Therefore, the probability of award should be a negative function of the community's marginal inducement cost, but a positive function of the utility to the grantor of output in that community.

The problem in the second stage is to allocate the total appropriation Z among $n_1 \leqq n$ grant recipients. In so doing, the grantor simultaneously sets the price of each grant in terms of the local matching requirement. Reformulating (4), one can show that the optimum allocation must satisfy

$$U_i/U_j = [p_i(1 + 1/\eta_i]/[p_j(1 + 1/\eta_j)], \tag{5}$$

for all i, j in n_1. The term η, defined as $(dQ/dP \cdot P/Q)$, is the elasticity of the local offer curve. Rewriting (5) as

$$U_i/[p_i(1 + 1/\eta_i)] = U_j/[p_j(1 + 1/\eta_j)], \tag{6}$$

gives the rule that grants should be allocated so as to equate the ratio of the marginal utility of output to the marginal inducement cost for all grant recipients.

The implications of the level of aid model may be seen more clearly in figure 4. The upper part of the diagram shows the marginal inducement cost curves of community 1 and community 2 and the grantor's marginal valuation functions, as a function of output in the two communities. The lower part of the diagram indicates the relation between the grant award and the amount of output. Community 2 has both a lower average and a lower marginal inducement cost than community 1.[17] Hence, at any level of output, the cost to

---

17. Unit cost $C(Q)$ is assumed to be equal to 1 in both communities. Differences in marginal inducement cost stem solely from differences in local demand functions.

Figure 4

Marginal Inducement Cost and the Level of Aid.

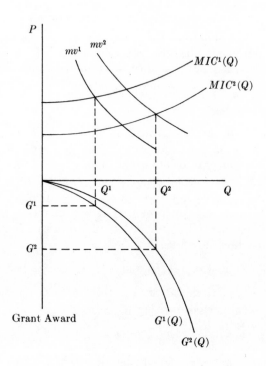

the grantor of inducing that output is lower in community 2. The grantor's marginal valuation of output, which declines with the level of output, is higher in community 2 than in 1. The equilibrium level of aid awarded in each community is determined by the intersection of the marginal inducement cost curve with the grantor's marginal valuation function. In figure 4, equilibrium occurs at (G^1, G^2). A lower marginal inducement cost is associated with a higher level of aid.

If the marginal valuation functions were reversed, so that $MV^1 \geq MV^2$ for any Q, then the equilibrium level of aid in community 1 would be greater than that in community 2. Thus, the model implies that, ceteris paribus, the lower the marginal inducement cost, the greater the level of aid. Second, the greater the marginal utility of output in any community, the greater the award of aid.

Testing the Grant-Award Model

In this section, an empirical test of the model of bureaucratic behavior is presented, using a particular project grant-in-aid. As indicated by the model, the specification of the award of aid is broken into two stages—the first the decision on which projects to fund, and the second the decision on the level of aid for those projects which are selected. The unit of analysis is the community, rather than the individual project. The first part of this section describes the data and the empirical specification. The second presents and interprets the results of the analysis.

Project selection data were collected for the Department of Housing and Urban Development's Basic Water and Sewer Facilities program, a small capital grant awarded directly to cities by the federal government.[18] The sample consisted of 430 cities, each of which applied for at least one water-sewer grant between 1966 and 1972.[19] Though some communities applied for and were awarded more than one grant during this period, all awards to a community are aggregated into a single dollar amount.

The decision rule for project selection given by equation (4) suggested a specification of the form

$$P(A \mid X, MIC) = f(X, MIC, N, Z) \qquad (7)$$

where

$$P(A \mid X, MIC) = \text{the conditional probability of award given } X \text{ and } MIC$$

---

18. Authorized as part of the Housing and Urban Development Act of 1965 (P.L. 89-117, 79 Stat. 451, Sec. 702), admissable projects under the program included storm and sanitary sewer systems, new water supply, water storage, water treatment plants, water transmission systems, and local distribution systems. Obligations were at a level of $150 million in fiscal year 1970 and 1971, the last year in which new commitments were undertaken. From 1966 to 1971, 1489 projects were funded or approved. The average award for cities in the sample was $604,030. Department of Housing and Urban Development (1972).

19. For a model of the decision to apply for project grants which draws on the same data source, see Chernick (1976), chapter 2.

X = a vector of community specific characteristics which determine the utility to the
grantor of a given level of output in the
community

MIC = the marginal inducement cost

N = number of applications submitted

Z = the total appropriation for the program

Equation (7) was estimated as a conditional logit model with a
dichotomous dependent variable.[20]

As in the award of aid equation, the level of aid should depend upon
a vector of community characteristics (x) influencing grantor utility,
the marginal inducement cost (MIC), the demand for aid (R), and
the total appropriation (Z). However, the direction of influence and
the significance of particular variables is not necessarily the same as
in the first equation. The equation is

$$g = f(X, MIC, R, Z) + e \qquad (8)$$

where

g = the level of aid per capita

R = the dollar amount of grant requests, per capita

e = the stochastic error term

In order to standardize for city size, the level of aid was measured on
a per capita basis. A linear functional form was chosen and the
equation was estimated using ordinary least squares. The sample for
the level of aid equation is restricted to the 237 sample cities awarded
at least one grant from 1966–1971. Because I analyze only a single
program, and do not break awards down by year, there is no variation
in Z and it is excluded from the final equation. Table 1 indicates the
independent variables tested in each equation, and their expected
signs. The variables are defined in table 2, along with a listing of
data sources.

---

20. See McFadden (1975) for a rigorous derivation of the necessary and
sufficient conditions for using the logistic model to estimate the selection prob-
abilities of a government bureau over a range of alternative choices. The logistic
model is

$$P(A = 1 \mid X) = \frac{1}{1 + e^{-X\beta}}$$

Table 1

SPECIFICATIONS OF THE GRANT AWARD MODEL AND
PREDICTED SIGNS

Independent Variable	Expected Sign Dependent Variable	
	AWARDUM	PGGRANT
MATCH	+	+
NUMAPP	+	NI*
OGAMTPC	NI*	+
CITYPCI	−	−
EFFORT	+	+
CITYPOP	+	−
DENSITY	−	−
POPCHG	+	+
AVGBPPC	+	+
CITYMAN	?	?
TYPGOV	?	?
CONGRESS	+	+

* Not included in specification.

The marginal inducement cost (MATCH) is measured as the
average, weighted by the dollar amount of each request, of proposed
local contribution rates for all applications submitted by each city.[21]
However, the share offered for each project gives only one point on
the local offer curve. Even for communities which submit several
projects, I am actually measuring an average inducement cost, rather
than the marginal inducement cost called for by the price discrimination model. Therefore, unless all communities have horizontal offer
curves—i.e., they will accept projects of any desired size at the

21. Cost variations across communities are assumed to derive completely
from differences in sharing functions. Because of a lack of data, differences in
costs stemming from differences in local production functions are ignored in
the empirical analysis.

By defining the price variable in terms of the local share, which is equal to
one minus the federal share, the expected sign on the price variable is positive,
rather than negative.

Table 2

EXPLANATION OF VARIABLES IN TABLE 1 AND DATA SOURCES

I. Explanation of Variables

AWARDUM = (1 if city awarded at least one grant from 1966–1971.
(0 otherwise.

PGGRANT = Water sewer grant award per capita, total 1966–1971.

MATCH = Average proposed matching rate for HUD water sewer grants defined as

$$\sum_{j=1}^{k} (\text{Local Contribution})_j \Big/ \sum_{j=1}^{k} (\text{Federal Contribution})_j,$$

where k is the total number of separate applications submitted by the city from 1966–1972.

NUMAPP = Number of separate applications for a HUD water sewer grant submitted from 1966–1971.

OGAMTPC = Total dollar amount of requests for HUD water sewer grants, per capita, 1966–1972.

CITYPCI = City per capita income, 1970.

EFFORT = City own revenue effort; (OWN REVENUE −.5*Ed.Exp.)/CITYPCI*CITYPOP)

CITYPOP = City population, 1970.

DENSITY = CITYPOP/Land Area, 1970.

POPCHG = Percentage change in population, 1960–1970.

AVGBPPC = Yearly average number of building permits per capita, 1966–1972.

CITYMAN = (1 if the city has a city manager form of government.
(0 otherwise.

TYPGOV = (1 if water and/or sewerage capital facilities are (provided by a general purpose government.
(0 if provided by a specific district.

CONGRESS = $\sum_{j=89}^{92} BC_j + APPR_j,$

Table 2—Continued

EXPLANATION OF VARIABLES IN TABLE 1 AND DATA SOURCES

where BC_j = 1 if city represented on House Banking and Currency Committee of jth Congress.

= 2 if represented on Housing Subcommittee of Banking and Currency Committee.

= 3 if represented by chairperson of Housing Subcommittee.

= 0 otherwise.

$APPR_j$ = 1 ⎫ same weighting scheme for House Appropriations.
2 ⎬ Committee; relevant subcommittee was Independent.
3 ⎪ Offices and Housing.
0 ⎭

DATA SOURCES: All data on HUD Water-Sewer grant applications and awards came from the Department of Housing and Urban Development Report Number M78 AECA, 1972. The special or general purpose governmental status of applicants was also derived from this report. Per capita income, and population were taken from the 1970 Census of Population (Economic and Social Characteristics), table 68. Our Revenue was compiled from General Revenue Sharing, February 1971, U.S. Department of the Treasury. [Actual compilations were performed by the Public Services Laboratory of Georgetown University. I am indebted to Dr. Selma Mushkin for making this data available to me.] Percentage change in population—1960–1970 came from the City and County Data Book, 1972. Congressional Representation was taken from the *Congressional Almanac*, selected volumes, 1965 to 1971. City manager status came from, "Recent Council-Manager Developments and Directory of Council-Manager Cities," International City Manager's Association, 1960. Building permits came from *U.S. Bureau of the Census, Construction Reports*, years 1967, 69, and 72.

proposed contribution rate—in which case marginal inducement cost is equal to average inducement cost, the price variable is misspecified.

The assumption made in this paper is that the average inducement cost as measured is correlated with a community's willingness to contribute to a project of a given size. If so, then within a certain range of the proposed project size, a higher proposed local share does imply a lower federal inducement cost.[22] This assumption implies that local elasticities of demand lie within some bounded range of one another.[23]

The number of separate requests for aid (NUMAPP) and the total amount of aid requested per capita (OGAMTPC) are additional measures of local demand for the aided output. Significant positive coefficients on either of these two variables would suggest a positive return to grantsmanship, and would also indicate that the grant awards are not exogenous to local behavior.

Grant awards depend not only on direct demand for aid, but also on community characteristics which influence the utility of output. One source of information about grantor utility is the published rating system designed to guide grant evaluators in ranking projects.[24] If program managers adhered to this system, then the probability of award should be a negative function of the community per capita income (CITYPCI). If considerations of fiscal equity help determine the utility function, then richer cities should also receive less aid per capita. A measure of the city's fiscal condition is its level of fiscal effort (EFFORT), defined as revenue from own sources as a fraction of community income. Though there are no strong expectations for this variable, a concern for interjurisdictional equity might suggest a

---

22. Some evidence to support this assumption was obtained in an analysis of the determination of matching rates in the price discrimination model. In a multivariate regression model, the proposed matching rate was found to have a highly significant positive effect in explaining variations in the final matching rates for funded projects. See Chernick (1978).

23. (a) If one community had a perfectly inelastic offer curve, while a second had a perfectly elastic offer curve, then, ceteris paribus, grant awards would favor the second community, even though its proposed contribution rate was lower.

(b) Though MATCH will have the correct sign under this assumption, the estimated coefficient on the price term may be biased by the use of average rather than marginal price. However, the direction of bias is difficult to ascertain without additional information on the conditional distribution of elasticities of offer curves, given observed average values.

It is clear that additional testing is required to determine the extent to which marginal inducement costs vary across communities, and the extent to which better empirical measures of such costs would support the price discrimination model of bureaucratic behavior.

24. This rating system is described in Vancil (no date).

positive relationship between effort and both the award and the level of aid.

While the probability of award should be a positive function of city population (CITYPOP), if the marginal utility of extra output in a particular community declines rapidly, larger cities should receive less aid on a per capita basis. Grantor utility is expected to be a positive function of local need for water and sewer facilities, measured by density (DENSITY), the rate of growth of population (POPCHG), and the rate of new construction as measured by the number of building permits issued (AVGBPPC).

Two variables characterizing the form of local government were also tested. The first was a city manager variable, designed to test whether city manager cities were more adept at grantsmanship than other types of cities. The second was a general purpose versus a special-district dummy (TYPGOV), to test the contention that project grants create bureaucratic links across layers of government which tend to reduce the power of local elected officials. Finally, community political power in Washington was measured by the degree of representation on the relevant congressional committee (CONGRESS).

The estimated equations are presented in table 3. Exclusion of particular variables was based on statistical significance. The price variable, (MATCH) has the expected sign in both equations, but is statistically significant only in the second.[25] These equations and other tests not presented here (see Chernick 1976), imply that the local inducement cost was not a factor influencing project selection, but that it did affect levels of aid. Evaluated at the mean, a 10 percent increase in the local contribution rate implied a 4 percent increase in aid. Thus support is provided for the hypothesis that in distributing

---

25. If the error terms in the probability of award equation and the level of award equation are not independently distributed, then OLS estimates of the latter, based on the sample of communities awarded a non-zero level of aid, yield biased coefficients (Heckman, 1976). In particular, such a correlation creates the possibility that a coefficient estimated by OLS may be statistically significant in determining the level of award, while its true role is to influence only the probability of award decision. On the other hand, if a variable is insignificant in the dichotomous equation, but is significant in the continuous equation, as is the case in this model, then it is unlikely that the estimated relationship in the second equation is completely spurious.

Table 3

ESTIMATED EQUATIONS FOR THE AWARD OF AID

Award of Aid (AWARDUM)

Method of Estimation	*Dep. Vble.*	*Ind. Vble.*	*Coefficient*	*Asymptotic t ratio*
MLE of	AWARDUM	MATCH	.03	(.36)
Dichot-		NUMAPP*	.17	(3.02)
omous Logit		CITYPCI*	−.0003	(−3.04)
		EFFORT	−.58	(−.08)
		CITYPOP*	.000002	(2.39)
		DENSITY	.00005	(−.74)
		POPCHG	−.002	(−.93)
		CITYMAN	.32	(1.50)
		TYPGOV	.47	(1.46)

* Significant at the .01 level.

Chi-Square of Estimate: (8 D.F.) 50.473
Sample Restriction: Cities that applied for at least one water-sewer grant from
                    1966–1972
Number of Observations: 430.
Percent Awarded Aid: 55.1 percent.

Per Capita Levels of Aid (PCGRANT)

Method of Estimation	*Dep. Vble.*	*Ind. Vble.*	*Coefficient*	*(t-value)*
OLS	PC GRANT	MATCH*	5.84	(4.60)
		OGAMTPC*	.39	(18.67)
		CITYPCI*	−.005	(−2.54)
		EFFORT*	−295.67	(−3.56)
		CITYPOP	−.0000001	(−.05)
		DENSITY	−.00002	(−.09)
		TYPGOV	−4.18	(−.82)
		INTERCEPT*	20.97	(2.45)

* Significant at the .01 level.

R^2: .6332   SEE: 18.76
Sample Restriction: Cities receiving at least one Water-Sewer grant from 1966–
                    1971.
Number of Observations: 237.
Mean Award: $20.69 per capita.

aid the federal 'project grant administrator behaves as an output maximizer.[26]

Additional results may be noted briefly. The negative coefficients for per capita income in both equations suggest that fiscal equalization was an important criterion in the award of aid.[27] The significant positive coefficients on the number of applications submitted (NUMAPP) in the award equation and on the level of requests (OGAMTPC) in the level of aid equation may indicate a positive return to grantsmanship. The results also imply that the level of aid is endogenous to local behavior. If the level of requests for aid is determined by local expenditures on the aided output, then the significance of the request variables suggests a possible simultaneity in the determination of grants and local expenditures. If this were the case, then single equation models of local public expenditures in which federal project grants are included as an independent variable may be misspecified.[28]

The larger the city, the more likely it is to be awarded a grant. However, CITYPOP has a negative, but statistically insignificant coefficient in the level of aid equation. Additional inspection of the relation between per capita awards and city size suggests that the true relationship is given by a third degree polynomial, thus explaining the insignificance of CITYPOP in the level of aid equation. Only very large and very small cities received proportionally less aid than their

---

26. A possible explanation for this pattern of significance has been suggested by Robert Inman. In the grant award stage, the grantor is constrained by the formal rating system and the relative visibility of the process. Since there is no legal basis for price discrimination, the grantor becomes politically vulnerable to charges of favoritism in the award of aid. The second stage, in which the level of aid is determined, is considerably less visible, and there is no equivalent to the formal rating system for project selection. In the process of negotiation with each community, there is more latitude for discretionary behavior by the grantor, and it is in this stage that price discrimination occurs.

27. The degree of equalization compares favorably with the results of at least one study of general revenue sharing. See Biederman (1972). The equalization results are further strengthened by the finding that richer communities are less likely to apply for aid. See Chernick (1976) chap. 2.

28. See O'Brien (1972) for an example of this type of specification. Our results provide some evidence for a hypothesis first suggested by Inman (1972), namely that for the microanalysis of individual city expenditures (rather than state-local aggregates), project grants cannot be viewed as endogenous, because localities can choose whether and how often to apply, and how much to request.

share of the population. This result is interpreted to reflect the nature of political coalitions in the United States Congress. The "something for everyone" criteria, implying a negative second derivative of the utility function, is strong enough to penalize the largest cities in per capita levels of aid.[29]

Measures of political influence are noticeably absent from the final specification of the award or the level of aid equations. I found no consistent evidence of specific congressional influence in determining the allocation of Water and Sewer grants. To provide some comparative evidence, the role of congressional influence in the award of urban renewal grants was also examined. In this program, which was reported out of the same subcommittee and administered by the same agency as the Water and Sewer grant, a statistically significant political influence was found.[30]

Two possible factors in explaining this difference in the role of political influence relate to the size of individual awards and to the size of the coalition supporting the program. Because Water and Sewer grants were quite small relative to Urban Renewal grants, the payoff to a congressman for the use of political influence was likely to be quite small relative to the cost in terms of depletion of "political" capital.[31] Second, the broad degree of support for the Water and Sewer program may have obviated the need to purchase support from a particular congressman in the form of grant awards. In such a case, where there is a great deal of demand for the grant, and its goals are unambiguous and widely supported in Congress, the most effective budget maximizing strategy is to reward as many congressional districts as possible. By contrast, the Urban Renewal program was among the most controversial federal programs ever enacted, implying a need to reward influential congressional representatives in order to insure continuation and expansion of funding.

---

29. A similar pattern was found in the relation between city size and the distribution both of Urban Renewal grants and the aggregate of all federal to local project grants. These findings suggest that results from the Water-Sewer grant are quite general. See Chernick (1976), appendix B-1.

30. See Chernick (1976), appendix B-II. However, the political variables still explained only a relatively small portion of the variance in urban renewal grants.

31. For a definition of political capital, see Williamson (1967). For a discussion of the politician as entrepreneur and ombudsman, see Margolis (1974), and Stockman (1975).

Summary and Conclusions

This paper has examined the implications of distributing inter-governmental aid in the form of categorical project grants. The basic argument is that when government bureaucrats are given the authority to allocate grants on a discretionary project-by-project basis, a market-like price-rationing mechanism supplants the pure administrative rationing mechanism. A utility maximizing model was developed, the implication of which is that the grantor discriminates between communities on the basis of local willingness to pay for federal aid, in order to maximize output induced per dollar of federal expenditures. A two-stage model of the award of aid was tested using the HUD Basic Water and Sewer grant, and it was shown that among communities selected to receive aid, those willing to pay higher matching rates per dollar of federal support were favored in the level of aid received. However, willingness to pay did not appear to be a determinant of project selection. The inference is that the discretion-ary behavior model posited in this paper is most relevant in the individual negotiation phase of project aid distribution, the phase in which the exact specification of each federal-local contract is determined.

In the empirical analysis, the distribution of aid was also shown to depend on the number and dollar amount of local requests, implying that the level of project aid was not exogenous to local behavior. This result may in turn imply a simultaneous determination of local expenditures and project aid for certain cities, with important consequences for the microanalysis of the expenditure effects for intergovernmental grants. Tests for such simultaneity are a useful area for future research. Potentially adverse distributional implications of price discriminatory behavior were counter-acted by a strong preference for interjurisdictional equity, with the result that a significant degree of equalization was observed in the distribution of Water and Sewer grants.

While this paper has not considered the full allocational and distributional implications of price discrimination, the results are suggestive of the possibly expenditive-maximizing features of an administrative mechanism for allocating grants-in-aid. It is recognized that the empirical results are based on a single, relatively small program. More extensive empirical testing of other project grant

programs, and comparison with other forms of intergovernmental aid
are required to determine the general applicability of the price
discrimination model. However, it is hoped that even this preliminary
testing will deepen our insight into the complexities of the intergovernmental allocation process, and serve as a brief for further
exploration, on a disaggregated basis, of the allocational effects of
administrative discretion in a system of fiscal federalism.

REFERENCES

(ACIR) Advisory Commission on Intergovernmental Relations. 1967. *Fiscal
Balance in the American Federal System.* vol. I. Washington, D.C.

Biederman, Kenneth R. 1974. "Patterns in State Aid Distribution," in *Services
To People, State, and National Urban Strategies; Part Two: State Aids for Hu-
man Services in a Federal System.* Ed. Selma J. Mushkin. Washington: Public
Services Laboratory, Georgetown University.

Breton, Albert, and Wintrobe, Ronald. Feb. 1975. The Equilibrium Size of a
Budget-Maximizing Bureau: A Note on Niskanen's Theory of Bureaucracy.
Journal of Political Economy.

Chernick, Howard. 1976. The Economics of Bureaucratic Behavior: An Application to the Allocation of Federal Project Grants. Unpublished doctoral dissertation, University of Pennsylvania.

————. 1978. A Model of Price Discrimination in the Determination of Federal
Matching Rates. Mimeo.

Department of Housing and Urban Development. 1972. Report Number
M78AECA.

Downs, Anthony. 1967. *Inside Bureaucracy.* Boston, Mass.: Little, Brown.

Gramlich, E. M. 1969. The Effect of Federal Grants on State-Local Expenditures: A Review of the Econometric Literature. *National Tax Association
Papers and Proceedings.* Columbus, Ohio.

————. 1977. Intergovernmental Grants: A Review of the Empirical Literature.
In Wallace Oats, ed. *The Political Economy of Fiscal Federalism,* Lexington,
Mass.: Lexington Books.

Gramlich, E. M., and Galper, H. 1973. State and Local Fiscal Behavior and
Federal Grant Policy. *Brookings Papers on Economic Activity.* Washington,
D.C.

Heckman, James. 1976. The Common Structure of Statistical Models of Trunca-
tion, Sample Selection, and Limited Dependent Variables and a Simple Estimation for Such Models. *Annals of Economic and Social Measurement,* vol. 5,
no. 4.

Inman, Robert. 1971. Four Essays on Fiscal Federalism. Unpublished Ph.D.
dissertation, Harvard University.

————. 1972. (1) The Structure of Urban Grants-in-Aid: 1957–1967, and (2) On
Specifying the Grants-in-Aid Variable: Gramlich, O'Brein and Simultaneity
Once Again. Fels Discussion Paper No. 18. Fels Center of Government, Univer-
sity of Pennsylvania.

McFadden, Daniel. Winter 1975. The Revealed Preferences of a Government Bureaucracy Theory. *Bell Journal of Economics*.

McGuire, Martin, and Garn, Harvey. Feb. 1969. Problems in the Cooperative Allocation of Public Expenditures. *Quarterly Journal of Economics*.

Margolis, Julius. 1974. Public Politics for Private Profits: Urban Government. In *Redistribution Through Public Choice*, ed. Harold M. Hochman and George E. Peterson. New York: Columbia University Press.

Niskanen, William A., Jr. 1971. *Bureaucracy and Representative Government*. New York City: Aldine, Atherton.

O'Brien, Thomas. 1971. Grants-in-Aid: Some Further Answers. *National Tax Journal* vol. 21.

Schultze, C. May 1974. Sorting Out the Social Grant Programs: An Economist's Criteria. *American Economic Review*.

Stockman, David A. Spring 1975. The Social Pork Barrel. *The Public Interest*.

Tullock, Gordon. 1965. *The Politics of Bureaucracy*.

Vancil, Richard. n.d. Notes on the Rating System for Water and Sewer Projects. Prepared as a case for the Bureau of Training, United States Civil Service Commission, in cooperation with the Department of Housing and Urban Development.

Williamson, O. E. 1967. A Rational Theory of the Federal Budgetary Process. *Papers on Non-Market Decision Making, II*.

DISCUSSION OF HOWARD A. CHERNICK, "AN ECONOMIC MODEL OF THE DISTRIBUTION OF PROJECT GRANTS"

Helen F. Ladd, Discussant

Howard Chernick's study of categorical grants is motivated in part by the observation that the rate at which the federal government ends up matching local expenditures shows substantial variation across communities even when a single maximum matching rate for the categorical grant is set by legislation. In light of this observation, the author develops a price discrimination model to explain how federal bureaucratic grantors simultaneously determine the matching rates and the distribution across communities of the project grant funds. By explicitly focusing on the allocation of scarce project grant funds, the paper adds a significant, new perspective to the study of intergovernmental grants. For example, the postulated model implies that neither the amount of project aid nor the matching price is exogenous to the local community, a result that contrasts with the conventional assumption employed in analyzing the stimulative effects of intergovernmental aid. Although the normative implications of the model are not very well developed in the paper, a better understanding of how the allocation process works in practice should help us to design improved systems of intergovernmental aid in the future.

Chernick's model builds on the bureaucratic behavior models of Niskanen and others by assuming that the bureaucratic grantor behaves in a way consistent with maximization of his own utility

---

[Doctor Ladd is an Assistant Professor in the Department of City and Regional Planning at Harvard University.]

function. Since he is interested in the interaction between the bureaucrats and the grant recipients rather than the interaction between the bureaucrats and the legislature, Chernick treats the project grant budget as fixed and assumes that the bureaucrat's utility is a function of the output of the aided expenditure category in each community. Why the utility function should take this particular form is not spelled out and, in my view, is an area that could benefit from further elaboration. Presumably, the form of the utility function should relate somehow to the reward or incentive structure facing bureaucrats.[1]

Since the federal government is a monopolistic supplier of the project grants, the federal bureaucrat making the allocative decision faces demand curves for the aided function that are downward sloping with respect to the local price of the aided category, i.e., M_L where M_L is the local matching rate defined as local expenditures/total expenditures.[2] Of central importance to Chernick's model is the assumption that these demand curves differ across communities. For simplicity in exposition, Chernick has chosen to translate these demand curves into offer curves where the quantity of output consumed or "offered" by the community is an increasing function of the federal matching rate M_F defined as federal expenditures/total expenditures. Provided both that the demand or offer functions are characterized by differing elasticities across communities, and that differing matching rates can legally and politically be applied, utility maximization leads to price discrimination.

According to this model, the grantor allocates funds among communities so that the rate at which the grantor is willing to substitute output in one community for output in another community just equals the ratio of the marginal costs of inducing additional output in the two communities. Because of the upward sloping offer

---

1. See, for example, W. A. Niskanen, "Bureaucrats and Politicians," *Journal of Law and Economics*, vol. 18, no. 3 (December 1975). In this article, Niskanen demonstrates that budget maximization is consistent with utility maximization, provided utility is a function of the bureaucrat's income and the perquisites of his position.

2. For simplicity of exposition, I will assume throughout this discussion that costs are constant so that marginal and average costs are the same. In addition it is convenient to assume that the units of output are defined so that the cost per unit is $1.00. While Chernick's theoretical model uses a more general cost function, the empirical work implicitly makes the constant cost assumptions.

curves, the marginal inducement cost to the federal government of inducing more output in a community exceeds the federal matching rate (M_F) that the grantor must pay. Specifically, the marginal inducement cost is the matching rate times the expression $(1 + 1/\eta)$ where η is the elasticity with respect to M_F of the community offer function.

Because of the analytic importance of the marginal inducement cost function, the elasticities of the community offer curves (or alternatively, the price elasticities of demand for the aided function) play a crucial role in the determination of the matching rates and the grant awards across communities. Unfortunately, Chernick presents no direct evidence from other theoretical or empirical sources in support of the hypothesis that these elasticities vary across communities. In a section of the larger study not included in this paper, the author reports a series of statistical tests that he interprets as support for the price discrimination model.[3] While I find these indirect tests supportive of the basic notion of upward sloping offer functions, the interpretation that they imply offer functions with differing elasticities is less compelling. Even assuming that Chernick's interpretation of the indirect tests is correct, however, more direct knowledge is required if one wants to evaluate the distributional implications of the price discrimination model. For example, do wealthy communities tend to have higher or lower price elasticities of demand for the aided function than do poor communities? Only with the answer to this and similar questions can the normative implications of the model be developed.

Having briefly commented on the theoretical aspects of the paper, I now turn to the empirical work. Chernick reports two equations based on water and sewer grants during the period 1966–72. The first equation uses a logit model to estimate the probability that a community will receive a grant and the second estimates the amount of the award for those communities receiving grants. The estimated equations yield some interesting conclusions, but the link between the theoretical model and the equation specifications is insufficiently developed.

---

3. Briefly, these indirect tests include the examination over time of the variance of final matching rates, the comparison of average matching rates across grant programs, and the correlation between proposed and final matching rates, controlling for city characteristics.

I will focus my comments on the matching price term, MATCH, defined as the average of the local matching rates proposed by each community during the period 1966–72.[4] Note that the implicit federal share (M^F) is simply one minus MATCH. While I find it reasonable to treat the average proposed matching rate (along with the associated grant request)[5] as one point on a community's offer function, the author's use of MATCH as a proxy for the marginal inducement cost to the grantor is open to criticism. As noted above, the marginal inducement cost is related to the federal matching rate by the expression $M_F (1 + 1/\eta)$ where η is the elasticity with respect to M_F of the local offer curve. Without further restrictions on the shapes of the offer functions, that would guarantee a positive correlation between M_F and the marginal inducement cost, the local matching share $(M_L = 1 - M_F)$ is an inadequate proxy for the marginal inducement cost.[6] In particular, this means that, in the absence of restrictions, the equations as currently specified do not test the hypothesis derived from the price discrimination model that either the probability of award or the size of the award is a decreasing function of the marginal cost of inducing additional output. To test the price discrimination model correctly, exogenous estimates of the elasticities of the community offer functions are required.

Chernick's decision to use MATCH as a proxy for marginal inducement cost is understandable. No other proxy is readily available. Furthermore, its behavior in the grant size equation is consistent

---

4. When calculating proposed matching rates, Chernick relies exclusively on dollar amounts, making no distinction between that part of the local share devoted to the provision of infrastructure that might have been provided even in the absence of the grant and the remainder. In developing the normative implications of the model, it would be useful to try to distinguish "soft" matches from hard.

5. Note that $M_F \cdot Q = G$ where M_F is the proposed federal matching shared (equals the proposed federal price per unit of output since costs per unit are assumed to be \$1), Q is quantity of output, and G is the grant request. Knowledge of M_F and G implies knowledge of Q and, hence, a point of the offer function.

6. Note that equality of the marginal inducement costs is an equilibrium outcome of the model for any two communities whose output is equally valued by the grantor. This implies that, at the equilibrium solution, M_F and the elasticity of the offer function will be positively correlated. This is an equilibrium result, however, rather than a statement about the relationship between M_F and the marginal inducement costs along any one offer curve.

with the behavior predicted by the model for the true variable. In light of this consistency, restrictions on the offer curves that will assure a positive correlation deserve to be specified.

The assumption of constant elasticity offer functions provides a convenient and conceptually simple restriction that yields the desired result in the context of the estimated regression equations. This can be demonstrated as follows. With the restriction that offer curves are characterized by constant elasticity, one point on an offer curve defines the entire curve. In addition, if the marginal cost to the grantor of inducing output in one community is higher than in another community for any output level, it will be higher for all output levels. In general, however, the observation that the grant request price (M_F) of one community exceeds the price offered by a second community is not sufficient to imply that the marginal inducement cost function of the first lies above that of the second. A positive correlation between the offer price and the relative position of the marginal inducement cost function requires a further restriction, namely that the community with the more elastic offer function propose a lower matching federal share than the community with the more inelastic offer function. Fortunately, Chernick's specification, in which he controls for the size of the grant request, assures this relationship. Since M_F is defined such that $G = M_F Q$ where G is the grant request and Q is total output, controlling for G forces an inverse relationship between the proposed matching rate and the output level offered by differing communities. This inverse relationship plus the fact that a single M_F and Q combination fully defines the offer function and its elasticity means that the federal share proposed by a community is necessarily negatively related to the elasticity of the offer function and consequently, positively related to the marginal inducement cost function. Thus, if we are willing to believe that the offer functions are constant elasticity functions, we can accept Chernick's interpretation that MATCH (or more correctly, one minus MATCH) is a proxy for the true marginal inducement cost.

This leads me to my final comment. In the equation explaining the probability of award in contrast to the size of the award, the coefficient of MATCH is statistically insignificant. One plausible explanation for this difference across equations was provided at the conference. Bureaucratic grantors may be less willing to use price differences to determine which communities are awarded grants than to determine the amount of the grant. Since the bureaucrat must be able to respond in terms of objective criteria to the congressmen whose districts did not receive federal grants, he cannot use the proposed matching rate as a criterion at the recipient selection stage. Only after the grant recipients have been selected is there leeway for the bureaucratic utility maximization and its implications for price manipulation that have been discussed above. While I find this explanation appealing, the thrust of my previous comments suggests another possible interpretation. MATCH may not be a sufficiently good proxy for the marginal inducement costs to pick up the price discrimination effects hypothesized in the model.

In summary, Chernick's paper provides some important new insights into the grant making process. His approach is an interesting one, worth further investigation. To make the results more useful to policy makers, a desirable next step would be to develop the normative implications of the model.

"REFORMING THE GRANTS SYSTEM"

Rudolph G. Penner

Introduction

The longevity of inefficient government programs is legend. Nothing seems more difficult than to get rid of bad programs in the face of entrenched opposition by special interest groups. Yet, there is one broad area in which we have disposed of a large number of programs in recent years. Urban renewal, model cities, various employment training programs, and numerous other categorical grant programs have been swallowed up by consolidated block grants. Some may argue that this does not represent much of an improvement in the allocation of resources, because not all of the consolidated programs were clearly inefficient. It is also debatable whether total government spending has gone up or down as a result. However, this paper argues that there is much to be said for consolidations, primarily because they seem to be a politically feasible way to get rid of some highly dubious programs.[1]

In all federal assistance programs, special interest groups gain much

---

[The author is a member of the American Enterprise Institute.]

1. This paper represents an expansion of chapter 10 of my *The 1978 Budget in Transition: From Ford to Carter to Congress,* (Washington, D.C.: American Enterprise Institute, 1977). I would like to thank George Vurdelja who acted as my research assistant during the preparation of this paper. I would also like to thank Richard Nathan and the attendees of the COUPE Conference for their helpful criticisms without implicating them in any conclusions of the paper.

of their power through the development of very close relationships with the members of specific subcommittees of the Congress. The subcommittees become the advocates for specific groups of recipients and providers and can gain them programs through vote trading and other devices. This process is responsible for the development of both grant and nongrant programs, but the politics of grants to state and local governments differs significantly from the politics of nongrant assistance in that it involves an extra set of fairly powerful participants—the governors and mayors. Governors and mayors obviously are also influenced strongly by special interest groups, but these are likely to differ in their relative power in different states and localities and, more generally, to differ from the groups that are predominant at the federal level. A natural set of tensions evolves with the governors and mayors wanting more freedom to serve their constituencies in vote maximizing ways while particular sets of Congressmen desire the ability afforded by categorical grants to focus aid on their favorite client groups. These tensions can be the catalyst for reform, although it should never be implied that reform is easy.

Before exploring areas of potential reform in more detail, it is useful to look at the recent evolution of the grant system and to explore some of its macro characteristics.

The Grant System in the Aggregate

As the following table shows, grants-in-aid grew rapidly between the early 1950s and the early 1970s, both as a share of the federal budget and relative to state and local expenditures. Between 1973 and 1976 there was a leveling off in both measures.

In fiscal 1977 and 1978, the relative importance of grants soared, but this was almost entirely the result of President Carter's short-run economic stimulus program, a large part of which was financed by the grant system. This was intended to be a temporary program, but localities have quickly become dependent on the funds and it has not proved easy to let it end on schedule. Much also depends on the congressional reaction to the President's welfare proposals which retain and add to the public service employment portion of the "temporary" stimulus package while increasing the federal share of total welfare expenditures in the long run.

Since the early fifties, the composition of grants has also changed

Table 1

HISTORICAL TREND OF FEDERAL GRANT-IN-AID OUTLAYS

(Dollar amounts in billions)

		Composition of Grants		Grants as a percent of:	
Fiscal Year	*Grants*	*Payments to Individuals*	*Other*	*Federal Outlays*	*State and[a] Local Expenditure*
1950	2.3	1.4	0.8	5.3	10.4
1955	3.2	1.8	1.4	4.7	10.1
1960	7.0	2.7	4.3	7.6	14.7
1965	10.9	4.0	7.0	9.2	15.3
1970	24.0	8.9	15.2	12.2	19.4
1971	28.1	10.8	17.3	13.3	19.9
1972	34.4	13.4	21.0	14.8	22.0
1973	41.8	13.1	28.7	17.0	24.3
1974	43.3	14.0	29.3	16.1	22.7
1975	49.7	16.1	33.6	15.3	23.2
1976	58.9	19.5	39.4	16.1	24.7
1977e	69.1	22.6	46.5	17.0	m.a.
1978e	81.2	25.1	56.1	17.5	m.a.

e = estimates.

[a] As defined in the national income accounts.

SOURCE: *Special Analyses Budget of the United States Government, Fiscal Year 1978.* p. 273, and *Mid-Session Review of the 1978 Budget*, p. 63.

significantly. At that time grants related to payments to individuals constituted over 60 percent of the total, and primarily consisted of public assistance programs such as AFDC and old age assistance. In the late fifties the interstate highway program increased the relative importance of the "other" category, and by 1960 payments to individuals fell to less than 40 percent of the total. After 1965, new transfer programs, such as Medicaid, prevented the payments to individuals category from falling further as a percentage of total grants, but after 1972 the relative importance of individual payments programs fell again to about a third of the total as general revenue sharing and other block grant programs added to the "other" category.

The change in composition also reflects the emergence of new priorities within the categorical portion of the system. For example, increased concern with the environment resulted in $2.4 billion in grants for sewage treatment plants in 1976 and this grant will grow rapidly to $4.4 billion in 1977 and $5.2 billion in 1978.

The composition also shifted because of the federalization of the public assistance programs for the blind, the disabled, and the aged in 1974. Since that time, this set of needs has been served directly from the federal government with the Supplemental Security Income program and is, therefore, no longer served by grants.

Since the late 1950s our grant system has tended to treat various states and regions more equally whether measured on a grants per capita basis or on grants as a percentage of state personal income. In part, this is due to the decline in the relative importance of highway grants and grants related to public lands. Both of these highly favor sparsely populated Western states, while the newer general assistance and block grants tend to distribute the federal largesse more equally.

The trend toward equality is shown in table 2.

The trend is particularly strong for the 48 contiguous states, but even after the disruption in the 1960s caused by including Alaska and Hawaii, there has been a pronounced move toward equality since 1967. A move toward equality measured by grants per capita or grants as a percentage of personal income obviously can be quite different from equalizing incomes among states.

The grant system as a whole has never played an important role in equalizing incomes among states. This is not surprising, since income redistribution is not the explicit goal of the vast majority of grant programs.

Table 3 shows that in 1967 and 1975 grants per capita were higher than the national average in *both* the five richest and the five poorest states, although there is a high degree of variance within both of these groups and in both years the majority of the top five states had per capita grants lower than the national averages. The relatively high grants per capita on average in the richest states did, however, fail to

Table 2

FEDERAL GRANTS: COEFFICIENTS OF VARIATION OVER STATES,
SELECTED YEARS

Calendar year	Grants per capita	Grants as a percent of Personal Income
1953	.443	.474
1957	.498	.526
Without Alaska and Hawaii		
1962	.431	.456
1967	.383	.432
1971	.285	.364
1975	.201	.261
With Alaska and Hawaii		
1962	.535	.499
1967	.747	.624
1971	.459	.430
1975	.356	.286

raise their grants as a percent of personal income above the national average whereas the ratio of grants to personal income in the five poorest was considerably higher than the national average in both years.

Consequently, it can be said that the grant system had a slight equalizing effect in both 1967 and 1975, at least as measured by a comparison of the five richest and poorest states. If anything, the equalizing effect was greater in 1967 than in 1975, although the difference is very small between the two years. Note that in 1967 grants per capita were considerably higher in the five poorest than in the five richest states whereas in 1975 they were about the same.

Putting the matter another way, the five poorest contained 6.2 percent of the population in 1967 and received 6.8 percent of total grants. In 1975 they contained 5.6 percent of the population and received 5.9 percent of total grants. Between 1967 and 1975, the share of the population in the five richest states went from 29.2 to

Table 3

GRANTS PER CAPITA AND GRANTS AS A PERCENTAGE
OF PERSONAL INCOME IN THE FIVE RICHEST AND
AND FIVE POOREST STATES, 1967 AND 1975

	Grants as Percent of Personal Income	Grants Per Capita
Five Richest States, 1967		
Connecticut	1.6	$ 62
New York	1.8	70
Illinois	1.5	56
California	3.2	118
New Jersey	1.3	48
Average, five richest	2.1	$ 80
National average	2.5	78
Five Poorest States, 1967		
Mississippi	4.7	$ 90
Arkansas	4.6	97
Alabama	4.0	87
South Carolina	2.7	59
West Virginia	4.4	103
Average, five poorest	4.0	$ 85
National average	2.5	78
Five Richest States, 1975		
Connecticut	2.8	$190
Delaware	3.4	226
Illinois	2.9	196
New Jersey	2.9	191
New York	4.2	276
Average, five richest	3.5	$230
National average	3.8	221
Five Poorest States, 1975		
Mississippi	6.1	$246
Arkansas	5.0	220
New Mexico	6.7	299
South Carolina	4.4	199
Alabama	4.9	223
Average, five poorest	5.2	$229
National average	3.8	221

18.2 percent, while the share of grants fell relatively less from 30.0 to 19.8 percent. However, later data may tell a different story, since 1975 was probably distorted by the effects of the recession.

At first sight, it appears as though the entire grant distribution is the result of a rather simple formula such as might be used for a single block grant. A very high r^2 can be obtained by regressing total grants received by states on only two variables—population, with the poverty population given a double weight, and tax effort. Without Alaska and Hawaii the relevant equation for 1975 is:

$$G = -1,253.5 + 0.2P + 76.8T \qquad r^2 = .97$$
$$(5.7) \qquad (38.5) \quad (5.5)$$

where G equals total grants; P is population plus the poverty population;[2] and T is tax effort measured by total taxes as a percent of personal income. I find the equation rather remarkable given the vast variety of formulae and the various types of project applications actually used to distribute grants.

However, it should not be oversold. It explains a large part of the variance in total grants for a very simple reason—larger states get a lot of grants while small states do not. It also makes some very large percentage errors in predicting the grants for particular states, especially for those states that are very small. For example, it predicts negative grants for New Hampshire and overpredicts Vermont and Nevada by more than 100 percent. In the unlikely event that anyone proposed consolidating our entire grant system and distributing funds according to a simple formula, even small percentage reductions in grants would create intense political opposition. This point applies with equal force to much more modest consolidations, and I shall return to this problem later.

Despite its flaws, the equation represents one way of indicating some obvious characteristics of our overall grant system. The very

---

2. State data on the poverty population was available only for census years when these estimates were made. Therefore, each state's poverty populations had to be estimated for 1975. This was done by fitting an equation to 1969 census data. The equation used the ratio of a state's per capita income to the national average in order to explain the percent of the population living in poverty relative to the national average. The resulting equation was used to distribute the 1975 poverty population. The data which has recently become available would not affect the estimates significantly.

fact that the size of a state is a prime determinant of its grant receipts indicates that there are not strong regional-specific biases in the system. For example, if the grant system were biased toward rural development the statistical relationships between population size and grant receipts would weaken. But the system contains grants specific both to rural activity and urban activity, and grants that can be enjoyed by both regions. In other words, in a system containing hundreds of different programs (the exact count is very sensitive to the definition of "program"), there is something for everyone, which is exactly what one would predict given the nature of our political system. While everyone can play in the grant game, the equation suggests that states with a higher tax effort do better, other things being equal. There are probably two reasons for this. First, and least important, the distribution of a small part of total grants (general revenue sharing) is directly linked to tax effort by the distribution formula. Second, tax effort can be taken as a crude measure of government activism in various states and activist states will, of course, attract more funds because of a willingness to engage in activities that are fully or partially funded by the grant system.

Since the 1950s there has also been an important shift in the distribution of grants between different levels of government. Twenty years ago, less than 10 percent of all grants went to localities. By 1975 the local ratio had soared to 28.6 percent and with the President's stimulus program it has probably risen significantly since that time. This development diminishes the usefulness of the above analysis of the distribution of grants over states since different cities within a state may be treated very differently. At the same time it is extremely difficult to study the distribution of grants among cities because of the great variety of governmental arrangements affecting the provision of grant-supported functions. For example, some cities are parts of counties while others such as New York and Baltimore are not. Such differences in arrangements can make it difficult to estimate the direct and indirect flow of grants to the particular geographical area contained within a city.

The geographic distribution of grants does not bear much direct relationship to the need for the reform of the grant system, except that reform is probably facilitated by the fact that grants tend to be so widely spread over states in a relatively simple way. This implies that if you consolidate a portion of the grant system and hold harmless those states or localities that particularly benefited from the categorical grants, the rest of the funds can be distributed with a simple formula without significantly disrupting the current overall grant distribution. As a result, there is much less potential for political controversy than there might have been twenty years ago.

The Potential for Reform

The intent of any public policy reform must be to improve the efficiency and/or the equity with which our system functions. Efficiency simply implies improving the quality and quantity of output for any given set of inputs. Within the context of the grant system and fiscal federalism, efficiency criteria demand the creation of behavioral incentives which induce states and localities to increase the production of those goods and services that are in the national interest. This generally implies increasing the production of those state and local public goods and services which provide beneficial spillovers outside of the jurisdiction having prime responsibility for the function in question. This, in turn, can be accomplished in theory with cost-sharing categorical grants where the federal cost share is chosen to reflect the importance of the spillovers being provided,[3] or with highly restricted block grants.

In this same context the search for equity can be interpreted as a desire to equalize the financial capacity of different jurisdictions to provide goods and services focused on the less fortunate in society. Economists often add the more stringent criterion that equals should be treated equally, but it is no easy matter to measure equality. Some would argue that our equity goals reflect just another type of externality. That is to say, each individual's utility function contains the utilities of other individuals and therefore each individual is willing to trade off some direct consumption to improve the lot of others.

The following discussion will describe categorical grants in the areas of nutrition, health, and education and will argue that they do not serve either efficiency or equity goals very well. Various responses

---

3. The relationship between cost-sharing grants and externalities is much more complex than this brief analysis makes it seem. See Alan Williams, "The Optical Provision of Public Goods in a System of Local Government," *Journal of Political Economy*, vol. 74, (Feb. 1966), pp. 18–33; and William Brainard and F. Trenery Dolbiar, "The Possibility of Oversupply of Local 'Public' Goods: A Critical Note," *Journal of Political Economy*, vol. 75, (Feb. 1967) pp. 86–90.

to this situation are possible. One can continually work for improvements in the structure of those categoricals that have promise and for the elimination of programs that are hopeless. But, as already noted, this approach runs head on into the opposition of the special interest groups who benefit from the status quo. It was earlier suggested that such opposition may be overcome if one enlists the governors and mayors in the cause of reform, but this cannot be done without bearing a cost, and that cost involves giving governors and mayors more freedom to allocate funds on the basis of their own political goals. This, in turn, can be accomplished by consolidating the categoricals so that they can be used for a wider array of functions.

One is immediately confronted with an obvious trade-off. With more freedom, the governors and mayors are less likely to concentrate on activities that have high beneficial spillovers. As will be noted later, not much may be lost compared to the present situation because the current categoricals do not seem to be designed to especially favor those activities with the highest spillovers. But it is, of course, impossible to prove rigorously that one could not have more success by attempting marginal reforms in the existing system than one will have with the more radical reform of consolidation.

There are, however, other efficiency considerations in assessing the merits of consolidation. It will be argued that the existing programs are often so narrowly focused that they cannot take advantage of economies of scale in their administration. It should therefore be possible to consolidate in a way that reduces the ratio of administrative costs to benefits.

It is more difficult to say whether decisions at the state or local level are in any sense "better" than at the federal level if one abstracts from the issue of spillovers. There can be endless arguments as to whether the lower levels of government are more or less corrupt or able than the federal government. Similarly, it is not clear whether the distortions caused by the activities of special interest groups are larger or smaller at any particular level of government.

It can, however, be noted that in the aggregate, grants are somewhat more important to state and local budgets than they are to the federal budgets. If lower levels of government are given more discretionary power, the disposition of grants may therefore receive more public and governmental scrutiny than is possible in the Congress. Moreover, in most areas of the country, local issues tend to get more press and media coverage than national issues involving domestic spending, and there is no better antidote for the distorting power of special interests than a better flow of information.

To the extent that state and local interest groups are less distorting than federal groups and to the extent that administrative costs can be lowered through consolidation, it should be possible to increase the final output of internal plus external benefits for given inputs. While there may, at the same time, be some loss in the ratio of the spillovers to the internal benefits, the fall in the absolute value of the spillovers need not be very large and it is even possible that it will be increased as compared to that existing currently.

The probability of losing spillovers is reduced if the consolidations can be kept fairly modest. It should, therefore, be emphasized that the sort of consolidations to be advocated in subsequent sections of this paper are far from radical. Nothing like a consolidation into general revenue sharing is advocated. Instead, funds would be restricted to specific uses that are closely related to activities supported by current categoricals, such as child nutrition or disease control. Of course, consolidated block grants make it somewhat easier to substitute federal funds for local funds that would have served the same purpose, but such substitution also occurs to a lesser degree with narrower categoricals. The difference is one of degree and not one of kind.

Whether or not the cause of equity is better served through consolidation depends on the effectiveness of the restrictions imposed on the use of the block grant and on the choice of the formula used to distribute funds among jurisdictions. As with the quest for efficiency one faces difficult trade-offs and it is much easier to argue that the current system of categoricals has many deficiencies than it is to prove that hypothetical untried consolidations would do a superior job. However, it can be noted that our categorical system has become so complex that major costs are involved in learning about what is available and what sort of application is likely to be successful. This biases the flow of funds toward communities that are large enough to be able to afford skilled "grantsmen" and that are clever enough to use them effectively. This hardly serves the cause of equity.

But it is very difficult to estimate the quantitative significance of such features of the current system. Consequently, the potential reforms must be analyzed under conditions of great uncertainty. In fact, despite numerous studies, there is little agreement on the precise nature of some of the most rudimentary features of the impact of different types of grants on the economic behavior of state and local governments.[4]

The following analysis will focus on issues related to the present grant system in only three program areas—nutrition, health, and education. First, the general characteristics of programs in these areas will be explored, and second, I shall ask how former President Ford's more detailed proposals in these areas could have been made more appealing conceptually and politically.

Many of the problems in the social program area are intimately related to the evolution of the Great Society programs of the 1960s and early 1970s. The philosophy of the Great Society was dominated by the notion that redistribution goals should be pursued with in-kind programs. In-kind programs are inherently complicated because, by definition, they must be structured to increase the consumption of a particular good or service by a specified set of people. In addition, each creates two constituencies—the recipients and the providers. The lobbying of the latter often distorts programs so that they are less efficient and equitable in serving recipient's needs than they otherwise might be. For example, the lobbying of home builders has biased our housing programs toward serving housing needs with new construction when strong arguments can be made for making much more use of existing housing for serving these needs.[5]

In many cases, the in-kind philosophy has been carried to extremes in that the in-kind consumption has been focused on needs that become more and more narrowly defined. In my view it is in these cases that the potential for reform is greatest.

Our nutrition programs provide an excellent example of this phenomenon. The most important single nutrition program is the

---

4. A review of the literature on the effect of grants on state and local spending and tax patterns can be found in Advisory Commission on Intergovernmental Relations, *Federal Grants: Their Effects on State-Local Expenditures, Employment Levels, Wage Rates*, (Washington, D.C.: February 1977); and in Edward M. Gramlich, "Intergovernmental Grants: A Review of the Empirical Literature," in Wallace E. Oates, *The Political Economy of Fiscal Federalism*, (Lexington, Mass.: D.C. Heath, 1977), pp. 219–39.

5. It should be noted that most housing assistance occurs outside of the grant system, but the same phenomenon afflicts health delivery and other grant programs.

food stamp program. It is supposed to insure that no one is deprived of an adequate diet because of a lack of financial resources. To achieve this end, the degree of assistance varies inversely with net income and directly with family size. In other words, the program is explicitly structured to provide for needy children as well as adults. Yet, we also continue child nutrition grants.

There are 15 different programs in this group. Some, such as the basic cash and commodity school lunch programs are not income related and since they subsidize rich and poor alike do not precisely overlap with food stamps. However, there are a number of special assistance and milk programs which provide additional subsidies to children with family income less than 125 percent of the poverty line and which more closely coincide with the food stamp population. There are other grants for child care institutions which subsidize children from families whose income is less than 195 percent of the poverty line, and then there are some summer free lunches which are given to both rich and poor in communities where at least one-third of the families have incomes less than 195 percent of the poverty line. (This one allowed my children to enjoy free lunches at the Georgetown, D.C., playground where the average participating family must have been in the top 2 percent of the income distribution.) Needy children and mothers-to-be are also served by the Women, Infants and Children (WIC) program which provides supplemental food stamp vouchers and commodities for pregnant and nursing, low-income women.

This vast array of programs raises a very large number of fundamental questions. For example, given all of the programs focused on children should food stamp allotments depend on family size? Or given that food stamps do depend on family size would we not be better off adjusting the food stamp program in order to allow the use of food stamps to purchase school lunches and other meals prepared by institutions? Do some of the special needs, e.g. those of pregnant or nursing women, differ sufficiently from those of the rest of the population to warrant a specialized national program?

Such questions would arise in the best of circumstances where the programs served the entire eligible population. But they do not. Because of administrative problems and other considerations, many communities choose not to participate. As a result, there are 700,000 children from below poverty line families who are not served at all by any of these programs while in other communities rich children can receive layer upon layer of subsidies.

In addition to the array of special feeding programs for children, there are numerous special grant programs for the elderly. For example, hot meals are provided at community centers. Both low and high income elderly are served by many of the programs where they are offered, but only a tiny proportion of the total elderly population actually receives benefits.

The situation in health services delivery is very similar to that in the nutritional grant system. There is a core program for the disadvantaged—Medicaid—that is analogous to the food stamps program. In addition, there is Medicare, a broad based federal, non-grant program for the elderly which is not income-conditioned. Then, there are numerous specialized programs aimed at narrowly defined needs or population groups which may or may not be income related. There are health programs for migrants and merchant seamen; for immunizations and family planning; for neighborhood and mental health centers; and for the treatment of numerous specific diseases.

The same pattern is repeated for elementary and secondary education. A large grant for disadvantaged students is supplemented by numerous categorical grants aimed at highly specific problems, such as learning disabilities and particular handicaps.

One might argue that all of these programs should be consolidated into broad block grants. However, I would exempt food stamps and Medicaid from any consolidation. Needless to say, both of these programs contain important structural flaws and are themselves in need of reform, but I would leave the responsibility for structural reform at the federal level. I say this because I think that there is a widespread, although not universal belief, that the prime responsibility for income redistribution should remain with the federal government. Given that the nation has chosen to rely heavily on redistributions in kind, these two programs are crucial to this effort.

Therefore, I conclude that the federal government should not relax the restraints on their structure by embodying them in block grants. That is not to say that they should be completely federalized. The grant approach to Medicaid allows considerable interstate variability in benefits and definitions of eligibility, and one can make the philosophical judgment that states should have some freedom in reflecting their own values regarding income redistribution within a set of constraints and incentives designed at the federal level. Food stamp benefits and eligibility rules are more rigidly determined by the federal government, and there are good reasons for keeping the responsibility for program design at the federal level.

However, the case for consolidating the other nutrition, health, and education programs, other than food stamps and Medicaid, into block grants is very strong. A careful reader might say that to be consistent I should put grants for the educationally disadvantaged into the same category as food stamps and Medicaid, but funds for the educationally disadvantaged are already distributed on a formula basis and the program already resembles a block grant more than it resembles an entitlement program.

The case for consolidating narrower health, nutrition, and education programs can be made on both practical and conceptual grounds. Practically, many are so small that they often serve a very small proportion of the eligible population, and they provide good examples of programs that cannot take advantage of economies of scale in their administration. For example, the WIC program spends 20 percent of its funds on administration while costs per visit in some health centers is as high as $80. Because the programs are typically very small, smaller communities often do not find it worthwhile to employ grantsmen while larger communities may apply just to attract federal dollars regardless of the severity of a particular problem in their jurisdiction. As a result, the geographical distribution of a particular problem such as mental illness need not bear a strong relationship to the geographic distribution of a related grant such as those that finance mental health centers.

Some of these problems could be alleviated by greatly expanding the budgets for the smaller programs so that they could serve a higher proportion of the eligible population and take advantage of economies of scale. However, the chances of significantly higher spending in this era of stringent budgets is about as remote as the chances of eliminating the programs altogether.

Not all of the programs are small. The school lunch program is a notable exception. However, most have another feature which casts doubt on the appropriateness of using grants to finance them. Most are almost totally devoid of the externalities which can be used to justify cost-sharing grants. I would argue that the benefits provided by the nutrition programs are particularly localized unless one believes that externalities are created because citizens all possess an interpersonal utility function containing the utilities of the recipients of these programs. To justify our current array of nutritional programs, this utility function would have to be so complex as to be totally implausible.

The health grants to governments present a slightly more complex picture since it can be argued that they convey external benefits to the extent that they aid the control of communicable diseases. As noted earlier, a consolidation of categorical grants into a block grant would probably not discriminate between those activities that have beneficial health spillovers and those that do not, but it is also impossible to identify such discrimination in our present system of categoricals. A very large portion of total spending is directed to noncommunicable diseases such as cancer, mental illness, and sickle cell anemia. Admittedly, some goes to communicable problems such as tuberculosis, venereal disease, and Hansen's Disease, but I would argue that in designing a new block grant, it would not be worth the administrative costs of trying to differentiate various types of disease control according to their beneficial externalities.

Some would claim significant externalities for the activities financed by education grants, and others call education a "merit good"—whatever that may be. However, the current complex structure of education grants focuses support on highly localized problems related to learning disabilities, and other physical handicaps, as well as providing aid to the economically disadvantaged. A generalized block grant would provide the ability to attack educational problems as they are defined by the local community and may provide more beneficial spillovers than are provided by the current highly rigid grant structure.

It is easier to argue that the present system of categorical grants has many failings than it is to argue that a consolidation into block grants represents a superior solution to the problem. One way of attacking the issue is to examine the success or lack of success so far with the block grant approach. General revenue sharing, law enforcement assistance grants, comprehensive employment and training (CETA) block grants, and community development (CD) block grants all represent efforts to increase the decision-making power of lower levels of government. However, the first two did not consolidate an existing set of categorical grants, although they may have acted as substitutes for a further expansion of the categorical system. The CETA block grant did absorb a number of programs, but over time it has begun to look more and more like a categorical grant as the public service jobs component has become more important and as that component has become subject to more and more restrictions in an attempt to make it more effective at creating new employment. The CD block grant most closely resembles the sort of reform advocated in this paper. It has been intensively studied by Richard Nathan and his associates at Brookings and the following discussion will rely heavily on their analysis.[6]

Although it was signed by President Ford in 1974 all of the legislative activity lending to its passage occurred during the Nixon Administration. CD block grants absorbed grants for urban renewal, model cities, water and sewer facilities, open spaces, neighborhood facilities, rehabilitation loans, and public facility loans. While CD block grants provide considerably more freedom to state and local governments in allocating funds, they are far from free of restrictions and administrative costs. Communities must make applications which contain fairly elaborate community development and housing assistance plans.

One of the most difficult steps in developing a program is the design of a distribution formula. No formula can be perfectly equitable. Regardless of its form, the passage of reform legislation is often facilitated by a hold harmless provision that prevents any community from receiving less in the short run than it obtained from the consolidated categorical programs. This requirement may limit the improvement in equity resulting from the initial reform.

In the CD block grant distribution, 2 percent of the funds are distributed at the discretion of the Secretary of HUD. Of the remainder, 80 percent is allocated to metropolitan areas while the rest goes to nonmetropolitan areas. All communities are held harmless initially and once the hold harmless portion is allocated, the remaining metropolitan allocation is distributed by a formula. The hold harmless provision is gradually phased out and disappears in 1980. Originally, the formula involved population, overcrowded housing, and the poverty population (weighted twice). Recent amendments have provided a dual formula for distributing funds. Allocations are determined either by the old formula or a new one which includes

---

6. Richard P. Nathan and associates, *Block Grants for Community Development*, First Report on the Brookings Institute Monitoring Study, Prepared under Contract H-2323R, U.S. Department of Housing and Urban Development (Washington, D.C.: January 1977).

older housing and growth rates in order to divert more funds to the slow-growing Northeast.

During the bargaining over the formula and eligibility, suburban counties were able to exercize the political power that they derived from their growing populations and they will do better financially under the consolidated system than they did under the categorical programs which tended to be more narrowly focused on central cities. Most of the categoricals were developed in a time when central cities had more political clout. Now that suburban counties have grown relative to the central cities, it is fairly safe to predict that they would be equally successful in the bargaining over any future consolidation of nutrition, education, and health grants and that this will create opposition among those who feel our real social problems are concentrated in the central cities. However, this is not a very good reason for opposing consolidations because the same forces are very likely to be successful in modifying the categorical system so that more funds are diverted to the suburbs.

Any discussion of the impact of the CD block grant on spending patterns is hampered by the fact that it is extremely difficult to know what would have happened to the categorical programs in the absence of the consolidation. In the CD area, the criticism of urban renewal and model cities was growing and this may have curbed their growth in the absence of consolidation. While we seldom get rid of programs, cut backs are slightly more common, and, even more often, we let the real value of dubious programs erode by holding money appropriations constant.

However, if one is willing to assume that in the absence of reform the categorical programs would have remained constant in structure and real value, it does seem to follow that CD block grants had significant impacts on the functional distribution of spending as local priorities and decision processes took over from the federal processes. In Nathan's sample jurisdictions, only 27.9 percent of the CD block grant was used to maintain programs which had previously been funded by the consolidated categoricals. New spending programs absorbed 53.3 percent of the allocation, while "substitution" (tax reduction, lower borrowing, cash balances, and avoided tax increases) absorbed only 6.6 percent. The rest was used to maintain programs earlier funded locally or by grants not consolidated into the CD program, or could not be allocated by Nathan's investigators.

It is even more difficult to reach definitive conclusions about the impact of CD reform on the distribution of income, primarily because the distributional impact of the consolidated categoricals is far from clear. For example, the distributional impacts of the urban renewal program are enormously complex and probably varied greatly from project to project.

Nathan and his associates do make some judgments as to who benefits from CD block grants without making explicit comparisons to who benefited under the whole array of consolidated programs. Almost 52 percent of spending was assigned to moderate and low income groups while 25 percent was said to be "community wide/ nonincome specific." It can therefore be concluded that at least the lower part of the income distribution was not ignored by the CD block grants, although the Nathan study concludes that there was some shift away from investment in the poorest areas of communities.

In conclusion, it seems clear that CD block grants successfully shifted decision-making power from the federal level to local officials and that these officials manifested a different set of priorities from those implicit in the categorical grant system. To me, the most important point is that less than 30 percent of the funds were used to finance activities previously supported by the categorical system. It is hard for me to believe that the local decision makers, who have to run for office, shifted priorities so radically unless it was in the best interests of the community. It is also hard to see that the nation as a whole suffered as a result, since it is not readily apparent that the older activities had more important beneficial spillovers than the new activities. Indeed, the benefits from both would seem to be highly localized.

There may, however, be a more fundamental problem. The block grant concept allows local decision makers wide latitude to allocate dollars which were not raised with local taxes. This "representation without taxation" may provide local taxpayers with the illusion that local services are cheaper than they really are and since this cannot be justified by referring to beneficial spillovers, an unwarranted expansion of government activity may result.[7] Of course, the same result can follow from categorical programs.

---

7. For a discussion of the distorting effects of including a tax effort term in a block grant, see Darwin G. Johnson and Charles M. Mohan, "Revenue Sharing and the Supply of Public Goods," *National Tax Journal*, vol. 26, (June 1971), pp. 157–68.

For this reason, Governor Reagan argued for a purist solution in the 1976 primaries. He advocated eliminating virtually the whole grant-in-aid system and using the savings to provide federal tax cuts rather than block grants. However, the purist approach creates a larger number of net losers, whose howls of anguish quickly relegated the Reagan proposal to the same political graveyard containing the McGovern demogrant.

President Ford's Consolidation Proposals

President Ford sought to extend the CD block grant approach to child nutrition, health, and education in his 1977 and 1978 Budgets. His proposals did not provoke the same violent reaction engendered by the Reagan purist approach. Indeed, they provoked hardly any interest at all.

If the Ford proposals had only been designed to enhance local decision-making powers while ending a potpourri of dubious grant programs, they may have provoked more interest. Unfortunately, they also explicitly attempted to achieve both immediate and long-run budget savings and this destroyed their popularity with the Congress and state and local officials.

It is useful to examine the Ford proposals in more detail and to ask if they could be modified to make them more palatable politically.

CHILD NUTRITION

The Ford program would have consolidated 15 child nutrition programs. (see figure 1 for a list of the consolidated programs.) Without consolidation the programs were expected to spend about $3.3 billion in 1978. Ford's block grant would have provided only $2.2 billion. The saving was accomplished by making children from families above the poverty line ineligible for block grant assistance. The new grant's distribution would have been based on the number of needy children in a state. The formula distribution would thereby have provided assistance for the 700,000 poor children now ignored by the categorical programs.

While the elimination of programs which essentially tax the middle class and rich in order to subsidize the middle class and rich often has intellectual appeal, such reforms almost inevitably create a large class of net losers who make it extremely difficult to implement

Figure 1
FLOW OF CHILD NUTRITION DOLLARS

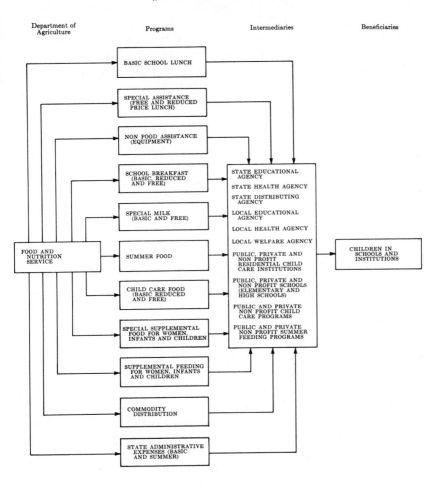

BEFORE—CATEGORICAL PROGRAMS
($3.2 BILLION IN OUTLAYS IN 1978)

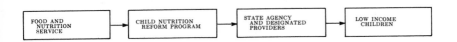

AFTER—CONSOLIDATED BLOCK GRANT
($2.2 BILLION ON OUTLAYS IN 1978)

the proposals. On the other hand any extension of the child nutrition programs to 700,000 extra needy children necessitated some reduction in subsidies to the middle class and rich or a budget increase—something Ford was unwilling to contemplate in 1977 and 1978. However, it may have been possible to gain considerably more political support by increasing the block grant budget authority toward the levels now represented by the 15 categoricals and by providing states with the ability to provide more assistance to nonneedy children albeit at slightly lower levels than they now receive. This could have alleviated one important disadvantage of the Ford program. By restricting eligibility to the poverty population he created an important income eligibility "notch" at the poverty line.

It is ironic to note that the consolidation of categoricals is often opposed by liberals who fear that the increase in the freedom given state and local officials would allow them to divert funds away from the needy. This particular Ford plan would have strongly encouraged a redistribution of income toward the needy, compared to that provided by the current system of categoricals, but it failed to gain any significant liberal support.

One might argue that the Ford plan did not go far enough in that it failed to consolidate the feeding programs for the elderly and other adults. These programs are particularly inefficient and inequitable, but they are also very small and spread out between Agriculture, the Community Services Administration and the Office of Human Development. Their inclusion would have provoked the hostility of elderly lobbying groups who have enormous political influence. Since so little money is involved, (far less than $100 million) the gain in efficiency from including such programs is probably not worth the increased political opposition which would jeopardize rationalizing the much more costly and important child nutrition programs.

HEALTH

The Ford proposal would have consolidated 20 health programs, including Medicaid, into a single block grant program with $13.2 billion in budget authority (see figure 2) in 1978. The funds would be distributed among states with a formula including the poverty population, tax-effort and per capita income.

Figure 2
FLOW OF FEDERAL HEALTH SERVICES DOLLARS

BEFORE CONSOLIDATION
($11.7 BILLION IN BUDGET AUTHORITY IN 1977)

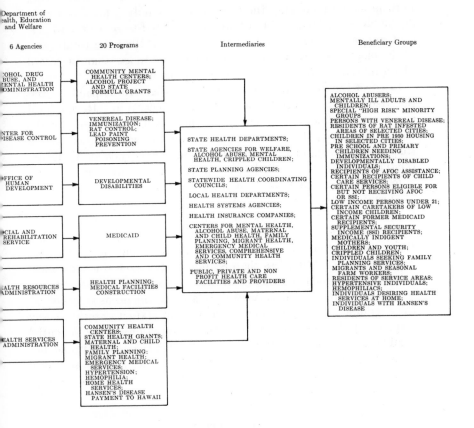

AFTER CONSOLIDATION
($13.2 BILLION IN BUDGET AUTHORITY IN 1978)

The proposal was dominated by Medicaid which was estimated to require $11.8 billion in budget authority in 1978. While the budget authority provided by the block grant in 1978 was approximately equal to the authority represented by the consolidated grants, the proposal was clearly intended to reduce outlays in the longer run. Ford proposed increasing the block grant by only 5 percent a year in the face of a Medicaid bill that was expected to soar at a 15 percent annual rate between 1977 and 1979. By 1980 the total value of the block grant would have been considerably less than projected Medicaid outlays in the absence of this program.

In effect the Ford proposal was a thinly disguised attempt to pass the Medicaid cost control problem from the federal to state and local governments. Since the federal government must bear much of the blame for soaring health costs because of the way its tax system treats health insurance and because of programs such as Medicare, the Ford program had little conceptual appeal. Moreover, it was noted previously that one can argue against the consolidation of Medicaid because it can be considered an inherent part of our national system of income redistribution.

There are, however, strong arguments for consolidating the other 19 health programs into a block grant arrangement. It would be a small program costing less than $2 billion, but now the categorical programs are focused very narrowly on particular diseases and specific population groups. As already argued, the needs attacked by these grants are sure to vary greatly from state to state; in any case, the programs serve only a tiny proportion of the potential eligible population; and it is hard to believe that there would not be large gains in efficiency and equity by allowing state and local authorities more freedom to allocate funds to the problems that are most serious in their own areas.

EDUCATION

Ford would have consolidated 23 different programs into one block grant with $3.8 billion in 1978. (See figure 3.) The block grant assistance was divided into four categories to insure that the handicapped and economically disadvantaged would still receive significant aid. The other two categories involved occupational education and library assistance. In effect, the 23 programs were consolidated into four mini-block grants. Budget authority was held constant at

Figure 3
FLOW OF FEDERAL EDUCATION DOLLARS

BEFORE CONSOLIDATION
($3.8 BILLION IN BUDGET AUTHORITY IN 1977)

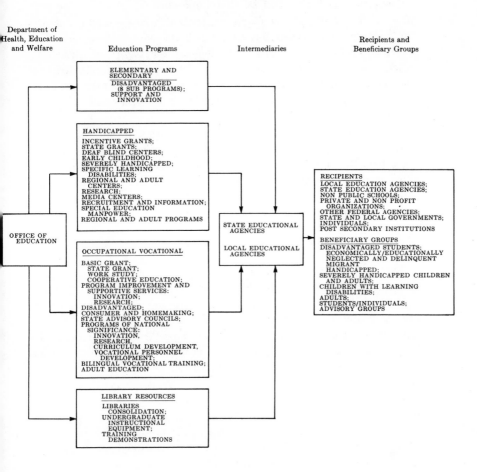

AFTER CONSOLIDATION
($3.8 BILLION IN BUDGET AUTHORITY IN 1978)

the level provided in 1977 and then it was proposed to increase funds at a rate of about 4 percent per year. In other words, the real value of outlays on these activities would probably have been eroded, but it is not clear how these grants will evolve in the absence of consolidation and the goal of this Ford consolidation was clearly aimed more at improving efficiency than it was at saving dollars. The current categoricals have many of the same conceptual and practical problems afflicting the 19 health categoricals discussed above, and in particular, they impose an enormous administrative load on state and local educational agencies by necessitating a huge volume of applications and burdensome record keeping and reporting requirements.

It is not clear to me why the Ford education proposals did not provoke more interest in that they did not involve the draconian budget cutting implicit in the health and child nutrition proposals. Some opposition may have resulted from the fact that the funds would have been given to state governments and there may have been a fear of major geographical redistributions within states.

Summary and Conclusions

The current grant system is so extraordinarily complex that it is virtually impossible to generalize about its content. However, one safe generalization is that it does contain numerous dubious programs. While it is much easier to make a negative case against the current categorical system than it is to prove beyond any doubt that consolidated block grants are better, modest consolidations seem to offer at least an opportunity to reduce administrative costs, to reduce the power of grantsmanship, and to serve local needs better without doing great harm to national goals of equity and efficiency. Of course block grants are not ideal and offer many opportunities for local inefficiency to replace national inefficiency. It was not the intent of this paper to describe an ideal set of policies. It only hoped to identify reforms that may be feasible within our complex system and that may, at the same time, offer enough hope for improvement to warrant an experiment.

This paper has concentrated on the characteristics of grant programs in nutrition, education and health, and has suggested that the Ford proposals which failed earlier might be easily modified to give them more political and conceptual appeal. But there are many other areas of the grant system that warrant examination. While it cannot be said that we have an explicit, coherent national growth policy, we do have an enormous number of grants aimed at "economic development." Some enhance rural development; others aim at urban areas; and still others are focused on particular regions, such as Appalachia. While greater simplicity and flexibility might be obtained through a consolidation of these activities into a major block grant, it is not even very clear what the goal of the block grant should be. It is obviously an area which deserves more thought and analysis.

One could go on to analyses of the potential for consolidating water resources grants, transportation grants, et cetera, and one could even consider using block grants to states and localities to substitute for assistance now given directly to individuals and private institutions. For example, housing assistance could be provided through local government even to a greater extent than it is today. However, these lines of inquiry will have to be pursued at a different time and in a different place.

DISCUSSION OF RUDOLPH G. PENNER, "REFORMING THE GRANTS SYSTEM"

Robert D. Reischauer, Discussant

The thesis of this paper—that a modest consolidation of the current grants system would be desirable—would generate fairly widespread agreement among the academic and public policy communities. The reasons for this, as this paper summarizes, are to be found in the weakness of the current grants system with its emphasis on categorical aids. The current system is thought to be overly complex. Its programs are often overlapping and duplicative. It is entangled in red tape. It is littered with small narrow-purpose programs, many of which don't work or are no longer relevant. It is inequitable in that many eligible governments and persons do not receive assistance, benefits seem to be distributed across the states with little relation to any measure of need, and it is susceptible to manipulation by grantsmanship. Furthermore, many of its programs are too restrictive and confining to conform to the various needs of different localities; in short, it is inefficient.

However, the litany of problems that supposedly afflicts the current grants system is often overstated. Increasing efficiency and great equity are not, as suggested in this paper, the only rationales for federal grants. While compensation for externalities or spillovers and redistribution are certainly the major forces behind most existing grants, there are several other dimensions which, in practice, have been important rationales for grants in the United States. First, the federal government has used grants as a mechanism for making state and localities provide services that national policy makers desire whether or not these services involve redistribution or spill-over effects. The recipients of such grants have operated as the federal government's agent. Such subcontracting of services usually reflects the fact that the states or localities are thought to be more capable of delivering the particular service. Second, grants have been used to stimulate innovations and experimental approaches to service delivery. Thus, the smallness of a grant program or its failure to cover all of those potentially eligible for the service is not an inexorable flaw. Unfortunately, such experimental grant programs tend to outlive their informational or innovational phases. A third, somewhat related, rationale for grants in the American system of fiscal federalism has been that of focusing national attention on a problem area. Whether the program is funded at a level sufficient to do the required job is often less important than the grant program's role in signaling that this is an area of national concern to which state, local, and private attention and resources should be devoted.

Moreover, even some of the admitted flaws of the current categorical structure have positive aspects. Some recipient decision makers have preferred the narrow earmarking of funds to special purposes because it has allowed them to pursue policies that would have been politically infeasible given their local interest group structure. Red tape and strings and the dominance of special interests and bureaucracies have probably had some effect in reducing the degree of fiscal substitution. A lack of funding sufficient to meet the nation's need in a problem area could be used to stimulate competition among potential recipients. Grants could be channeled to those areas that have both the most severe problems and the greatest willingness to do something about them. Some overlap and duplication can be rationalized both as providing back up systems in case of failure and as a method of testing different approaches where uncertainty exists. To be sure, most of these "silver linings" are not fully exploited in the current system.

Despite the added dimensions or rationales for grants, it is clear that there are many that serve no national function. However, as Penner points out, the case for consolidation, as opposed to elimination, is quite uncertain. This is because there is a great deal of ignorance concerning the effects of the current grant system, let alone any consolidation. One argument in favor of consolidation falls into the realm of political strategy: grant consolidation may be the only politically feasible way of eliminating many small, dubious programs that have outlived their usefulness. Supposedly the grip that special interests and selfish bureaucracies have on the narrow purpose grant programs and on the congressional subcommittees that control these programs could be broken by a consolidation strategy that would unleash the counterveiling force of mayors and governors who would be the recipients of the new consolidated block grants. While this logic may seem attractive, the history of the last decade's attempts to pursue such consolidation has not shown this strategy to be a highly successful one.

Penner has also argued that there are definite merits to consolidation irrespective of its political feasibility. The benefits included are that the inexorable growth of spending on narrow inefficient programs might best be reduced through consolidation strategy; that block grants could lead to a redirection of resources to more equitable ends; that consolidation could bring economies of scale and administrative cost savings; that efficiency would be served through consolidation because local rather than federal control over spending decisions will reflect better information flows, an ability to tailor programs to the specific needs of local areas, and a shift in decision-making power from specialized bureaucracies to the general voter.

It is possible that many of these benefits could be illusory or come at too high a cost. With respect to the costs, Penner has pointed out that emphasis on programs with spillover effects could very well be reduced if decision making were left to state or local officials as it would be under a block grant program. While simplifications might be expected from grant consolidation, the tendency of the Congress has been to add strings and introduce red tape to existing block grants programs after it has become apparant that state and local, rather than federal, priorities are being pursued. Not only have red tape and strings reappeared but also there has been a clear tendency to recategorize block grants and to spawn new categorical programs because the state and local spending decisions in the block grants program aren't meeting the national needs. The recent youth employment initiatives with respect to the CETA program and the Urban Development Action Grants (UDAGs) in the Community Development Block Grant (CDBG) program are examples of this.

The question whether consolidation will lead to a slower growth in expenditures for these programs is one that only history can answer. However, it appears that mayors and governors are every bit as facile at milking the relevant congressional committees for increased block grant assistance as were the special interest groups and specialized bureaucracies with respect to the narrow purpose grant programs.

Whether or not the distribution of consolidated programs will be more equitable than that of the more narrow grant programs is open to question. While the data presented in this paper show that the aggregate distribution of federal grants can be explained largely by population and tax factors, this is not at all true for subgroups of programs such as the nutrition, education, or health programs that Penner would like to consolidate. If the current distributions of these programs are at all related to measures of need, the distribution of the consolidated block grant is likely to be somewhat less equitable. This is because the Congress has tended to view block grant programs as revenue sharing and has shown a proclivity to equalize per capita distributions of assistance under block grants. This is understandable because the more diffuse and general a program objective—as is the case under block grants—the more difficult it is to defend wide grant variations among recipients. While the severity of many problems may not differ much among states, the recent grants history has been one of channeling federal aid directly to local governments where disparities are extremely wide.

These facts together with the experience of recent consolidations and block grant efforts—the Partnership for Health, CDBG, and CETA programs—suggest that while consolidation is attractive strategy it may generate new problems and not solve old ones. In short, consolidation may be going from one unappealing course to another. The positive case for consolidation and block grants can't consist solely of the case against categorical grants.

THE USE OF FEDERAL GRANTS FOR COUNTERCYCLICAL JOB CREATION

Roger J. Vaughan

1. Introduction

The precipitous decline in employment during 1974 and the first half of 1975, coupled with well publicized fiscal problems in many of the nation's largest cities, led to a rapid expansion in federal grants to local governments to create jobs. This response included the allocation of nearly $6 billion for public service jobs through grants made under Titles II and VI of the Comprehensive Employment and Training Act (CETA), and $6 billion in grants made under

NOTE: This paper draws heavily upon research conducted for the Economic Development Administration by the Rand Corporation. To date, three reports have been produced: Roger Vaughan, *Public Works as a Countercyclical Device: A Review of the Issues*, The Rand Corporation, R-1990-EDA, July 1976; Georges Vernez, Roger Vaughan, Burke Burright, and Sinclair Coleman, *Regional Cycles and Employment Effects of Public Works Investments*, The Rand Corporation, R-2052-EDA, January 1977; and Georges Vernez and Roger Vaughan, *Assessment of Countercyclical Public Works and Public Service Employment Programs*, The Rand Corporation, R-2214-EDA, Sept., 1978; and one paper, Georges Vernez, *Public Works as Countercyclical Fiscal Policy*, The Rand Corporation, P-5859, April 1977. I am indebted to Georges Vernez who has directed this research, and to Professors William Oakland and Peter Mieszkowski for many helpful comments and suggestions. However, the views expressed are my own and not those of the Rand Corporation or the Economic Development Administration.— Roger J. Vaughan, economist, the Rand Corporation.

the Local Public Works Acts (LPW) of 1976 and 1977.[1] With the possibility of a new bout of recession facing the country, it is timely to review the effectiveness of the last round of anti-recession grant policies.

Postwar experience with direct job-creating grant programs has been limited. Under the Accelerated Public Works Program about $1.7 billion was spent during FY 1962 and FY 1963. The Public Works Impact Program, (PWIP) enacted in response to the 1970 recession, disbursed only $130 million. Between 1972 and 1976, the Emergency Employment Act provided local governments with $1.6 billion to hire public employees.

Several considerations underlie the renewed emphasis on direct job creation through federal grants. First, the economic slowdown in 1974 was accompanied by double digit inflation, and it was hoped that a grant program, directed to those areas where unemployment and idle capacity were most severe, would result in less inflationary pressure than a more broadly applied fiscal policy such as a tax cut. Second, the severity of the recession had revealed sharp differences between areas—older cities in the Northeast suffered unemployment rates two or three times as high as those in sunbelt cities. It was hoped that a regionally targeted program—even if it had little aggregate stimulative effect—would afford some relief to the most depressed areas. Nor was the recession experienced with equal severity by all sectors or all groups in the labor force. Public works projects were aimed at the faltering construction and durable goods sectors, and public service jobs were subsidized to help target aid on the chronically unemployed. Third by channeling funds through local governments, the weak financial position of large cities could be bolstered, and cyclical local budget cutting could be avoided. Finally, the programs were viewed as furthering the redevelopment of central cities, whose chronic need for both public and private investment received wide publicity.

To justify the use of countercyclical public works and public service employment programs, rather than the alternative of a combination of tax cuts and other stimuli coupled with countercyclical revenue sharing, grants for those purposes must target on

---

1. The Local Public Works Act of July 1976 made $2 billion available for local public works, and the Public Works Employment Act of May 1977 made a further $4 billion available.

the areas that experience cycles most severely, and local government must use the grants to provide jobs for those workers—defined according to industry, occupation, or socioeconomic characteristics—rendered jobless through economic slowdown. This paper examines these two targeting issues: the ability to distribute funds in ways that reflect local cyclical needs is discussed in the first section, and the ability to encourage economic activities that absorb the cyclically unemployed is discussed in the second.

In addition to the difficulties of accurate targeting, there are a number of other problems implicit in these countercyclical programs which cannot be treated at length here but deserve mention.

First, increasing federal grants to a given area does not guarantee that local expenditure will increase by an amount equal to that grant. Federal funds may simply result in a reduction in local short-term borrowing that would otherwise have been undertaken to cover the recessionary short-fall in revenues.[2] To the extent that this happens, there will be little increase in employment.

Even if local employment does increase, this is by no means an unmixed blessing. The availability of federal funds may encourage cities to avoid making painful, but necessary, cutbacks. Many of the most troubled cities have a large share of their work forces in public employment (Peterson 1976) and have been reluctant to reduce municipal employment even in the face of declining population. The pattern of federal aid may have reinforced this tendency. Per capita federal aid has climbed from \$65 in FY 1976 to \$217 in FY 1978 in Cleveland, and from \$47 to \$251 in Newark. By contrast, Dallas received \$51 in FY 1976 and this had increased by only \$3 by FY 1978.

The allocation of grants may have other distorting effects. Many of the areas with high unemployment are growing slowly or are actually declining. Long-run economic development necessarily involves the movement of workers from declining to growing labor markets. To the extent that the promise of public service or construction jobs delays these migration decisions, economic recovery will encounter bottlenecks in the supply of labor in growth areas. The grants will have, in effect, shifted the national Phillips curve outward.

---

2. This issue is discussed by Courant, Gramlich, and Rubinfeld in the first paper in this volume.

A third problem is that, by focusing on short run, countercyclical, objectives, the ability of the programs to address long-run development goals may be impaired. Thus CETA funds are diverted from providing training and work experience for the chronically unemployed to subsidizing the employment of the relatively well-qualified municipal workers; and public works funds, whose goal is to provide the public infrastructure necessary for local development, are used for make-work projects with few long-run development impacts.

Regional Cyclical Behavior and the Distribution of Countercyclical Job-Creating Grants

Ideally, a targeted countercyclical program would distribute funds in a way that reflects the cyclical behavior of local areas. A number of allocation guidelines could be developed with respect to different aspects of local cycles:

Severity.[3] Funds would be concentrated in areas that experience severe cycles.

Timing.[4] Funds would be disbursed rapidly to areas that typically lead the nation, but only short-term projects should be undertaken, and the volume of funds should be reduced as the recession trough is passed. Long-term projects would be concentrated in areas that typically lag behind the nation, particularly during recovery.

Conformity.[5] If the cyclical behavior of an area conforms closely to that of the nation, then funds can be provided at the first indication of a national slowdown and reduced at the first indication of an upturn. Grants to areas which exhibit low conformity must be based upon local rather than national indicators.

---

3. Measured by the decline in employment, peak to trough, as a percentage of peak employment.

4. Timing can be measured with respect to cycle turning points, or with respect to fluctuations in monthly growth rates in local employment compared with those of the nation.

5. Conformity is measured as the extent to which local fluctuations in employment growth are explained by national fluctuations.

Responsiveness.[6] An area which is highly responsive to national changes should be the recipient of large grants during the downswing, but funds should be reduced during the upswing. Understanding "responsiveness" allows severity to be anticipated.

Duration.[7] Areas that are slow to return to their peak employment would receive large grants and would be encouraged to undertake long-term projects.

LOCAL CYCLICAL BEHAVIOR[8]

An examination of cyclical behavior in 147 labor market areas (LMAs) reveals a wide variation between different areas with respect to each of the cycle characteristics listed above.

Cycle severity has varied across LMAs from only 5 percent to as much as 19 percent. The average LMA experienced a cycle severity of about 5 percent. There is little consistency, from cycle to cycle, in the LMAs that experienced the most severe recessions. Many LMAs did not experience any decline in employment during national cycles. The number varies according to the severity of the national cycle: 59 LMAs had no absolute decline in employment during the mild 1960–1962; 40 LMAs in the 1970–1971 national cycle, and 20 LMAs experienced no decline in the 1974-present cycle. The areas that tend to skip the national cycles in each are characterized by rapid long-term employment growth and a low percentage of employment in manufacturing or a low proportion of manufacturing employment in durable goods. LMAs that are also state capitals are more likely to skip the national cycles than are other LMAs.

There are large variations among LMAs in the characteristics of their employment cycles in response to national economic fluctuations. The timing of turning points in different areas' employment cycles coincides with that of the nation in only a handful of cases.

---

6. Measured as the change in the local growth rate in response to a change in the national growth rate.

7. Measured as the time taken for local employment to return to its peak level.

8. Two analyses were conducted. One, using monthly time series of total employment, examined responsiveness, timing, and conformity in the relationship between local and national employment growth. The second analysis not only measured cycle characteristics—including severity and timing—and analyzed the regional patterns of these characteristics in each post-1960 recession, but also measured consistency from cycle to cycle (Vernez et al. 1977).

At initial downturns, the average LMA led the nation in recession by about three months and, at upturns, lagged the nation by two months. At the downturn of the 1974-to-present national cycle, the timing of turning points in LMA employment cycles ranged from a 16-month lead to a 3-month lag. This range has been greater during less severe national cycles. The use of past LMA timing patterns at turning points to predict the timing of the turning points of the following cycle would result in correct predictions in fewer than half of the cases.

In Chicago, more than half of the variance in monthly employment growth rates can be explained by changes in the national growth rate, and in Huntsville, Alabama, only 3 percent. A similar range is observable in area responsiveness. A one percentage point increase in the national growth rate is associated with a 3 percentage point change in the employment growth rate in Bay City, but with a less than 0.3 percentage point change in Tucson.

The return-to-peak duration of employment cycles ranged from less than a year to more than four years in all of the post-1960 national cycles. However, it exceeded 18 months in most areas, well above the average duration for most types of public works projects, and also above the average duration of most countercyclical public service jobs.

Nevertheless, some patterns do emerge. Regional patterns are discernible for some of these indicators and are summarized in table 1. LMAs in the old manufacturing belt tend to experience relatively severe cycles, slightly lagged behind the nation although conforming with the nation overall. Sunbelt areas tend to lead the nation and exhibit both low conformity and responsiveness.

There are also differences among types of area. Large LMAs tend neither to lead nor lag behind the nation but to conform closely to it, responding to a one percentage point change in the national growth rate with a similar change of about one percentage point. This behavior presumably signifies that the diverse economic structure reflects the nation as a whole more accurately than it does the structure of smaller areas. The former do *not* suffer severely from cycles—the high unemployment rate during the recent recession in many large cities appears to reflect secular rather than cyclical behavior.

Of the 48 LMAs that exhibit low conformity, 22 are also fairly unresponsive to the changes in the national rate of employ-

Table 1
SUMMARY OF LABOR MARKET CYCLICAL BEHAVIOR SINCE 1960, BY REGION

Region	*Severity*	*Timing*	*Conformity*	*Responsiveness*
New England	Mixed	Mixed	Low	Mixed
Middle Atlantic	High	Lag/Coincident	Close	Low
East-North-Central	Medium	Lag/Coincident	Close	High
West-North-Central	High	Lag	Mixed	Low
South Atlantic	Mixed	Lead	Low	Mixed
East-South-Central	Mixed	Lead	Low	Mixed
West-South-Central	Mixed	Lead	Mixed	Mixed
Mountain	Mixed	Lead	Very low	Very low
Pacific	Mixed	Lead	Mixed	North: High South: Low

ment growth, while only six are highly responsive. Because these 22 LMAs exhibit patterns of employment change that are independent of the national economy, they can be considered prime candidates for countercyclical public works projects during a national recession if a recovery is expected and if they have experienced a loss of employment. Of the 24 LMAs that conform closely to the national pattern, none exhibit low responses and 10 exhibit high responses. If a national recession is expected, countercyclical public works should be concentrated in these 10 LMAs and would experience a rapid and fairly large loss of jobs, since they are closely tied to the nation. Nonresponsive LMAs tend to be independent of the nation.

These findings have some implications for the distribution of countercyclical funds. During the early stages of a national recession, funds should be concentrated in large LMAs, and LMAs in the old manufacturing belt because there is a high probability that these areas will experience a decline in employment. As the recession progresses, a more pragmatic approach is called for, and grant allocations should be based upon local cyclical behavior. Overall, however, past behavior is a poor basis for the geographical allocation of countercyclical funds.

ALLOCATION OF COUNTERCYCLICAL JOB-CREATING GRANTS

The actual allocation of CETA and LPW funds has not corresponded closely with local cyclical needs. Nationally, in 1975 and 1976, allocations per cyclically unemployed person[9] were $454 under CETA, Title II, and $960 under CETA, Title VI. Corresponding allocations per unemployed person were $137 and $289, respectively. The variation from state to state was very large—larger per cyclically unemployed person than per noncyclically unemployed person. This is to be expected since the total unemployed rate is a guideline used in the allocation of funds. For example, Washington received $3640 under CETA, Title II, per cyclically unemployed person, while Kansas received only $52. Allocations per unemployed person in these two states were $223 and $29, respectively.

The ratios of standard deviation from the mean for allocations per cyclically unemployed person was 1.37 for CETA II and 1.04

9. Cyclical unemployment is measured as the decline in employment from local cycle peak to local cycle trough, 1974–75.

for CETA VI, indicating considerable inequality among states. With respect to allocations per unemployed person, the corresponding ratios were 0.64 and 0.27, indicating that program funds were more equally distributed among states with respect to total unemployment.

Under the PWIP program, $62 were allocated per cyclically unemployed person nationally, and $13 per unemployed per person. The corresponding allocations under round 1 of LPW are $740 per cyclically unemployed and $223 per unemployed, and under round 2, $2381 per cyclically unemployed and $1799 per unemployed. The range among states is considerable—Iowa received only $3 per unemployed under PWIP, while Arkansas received $55. Wyoming received $1263 per unemployed person under LPW round 1 allocations, Florida only $66.

The allocation among states is more equal with respect to total unemployed than with respect to cyclically unemployed for both PWIP and LPW funds, as was the case under both CETA, Title II, and CETA, Title VI. However, the ratios of standard deviation from the mean indicate generally greater inequality in allocation of funds to the states under the Local Public Works programs than under the CETA programs.

Other aspects of the regional distribution of countercyclical funds deserve attention. CETA funds have been concentrated in urban areas. In the 10 states receiving the highest absolute allocations under the CETA II and CETA VI programs, 80.7 percent and 79.4 percent of the population, respectively, lived in urban areas. The corresponding percentages in the 10 states receiving the smallest allocations of funds were 64.3 percent for CETA II and 56.0 percent for CETA VI. Large urban states, with a low share of their labor force in agriculture, have tended to experience cycles of greater than average amplitude and to be relatively responsive to cyclical fluctuations.

PWIP projects tended to be concentrated in small towns and rural areas. Areas with populations in excess of 500,000—in which nearly 16 percent of the nation's populations live—received less than two percent of the funds. Yet, large cities have proved highly responsive to cyclical changes in national employment growth. Allocations under Rounds 1 and 2 of LPW were much more heavily concentrated in large cities, with a third of all allocations going to places with populations in excess of 100,000.

It should be noted that not all the benefits of countercyclical programs are experienced in the area to which the funds are allocated. The local economy may not be able to meet the material and labor requirements of a program and may have to depend on other regions. These spillover effects from direct employment demands are likely to be relatively small for public service employment programs. Vacancies will be filled from the locally unemployed. For public works projects, spillovers will depend upon the extent to which the special skills required for the project are available in the local labor force. The greater the reliance on highly skilled workers, the more likely some of the demands will be met from outside the region.

Cycles and the Allocations of Countercyclical Grants among Sector and Labor Market Groups

Even within a given LMA, the effect of a recession is not felt equally by all industries, occupations, and socioeconomic groups. This section reviews the impact of cycles on different sectors and different groups in the labor force and the success of alternative countercyclical job-creating programs in providing employment for those groups most affected. To compare the characteristics of the cyclically unemployed with the characteristics of people hired under counter-cyclical programs suggests a number of ways in which targeting might be improved.

THE DISTRIBUTION OF CYCLICAL UNEMPLOYMENT

All sectors are not equally sensitive to changes in the national rate of employment growth. The manufacturing and construction sectors typically experience cycles of much higher amplitude than all sectors taken together. Finance, insurance and real estate (FIRE), mining, selected services, and the government sector are cyclically the least sensitive. Between November 1973 and June 1975, construction employment fell by 7.0 percent and manufacturing employment by 9.6 percent. By contrast, employment in mining rose by 17.6 percent; in finance, insurance, and real estate by 4.1 percent; and in services by 7.7 percent.

The construction sector is of particular importance, since the on-site labor demanded by public works projects must be provided largely by cyclically unemployed construction workers. Over the course of a cycle, the construction sector employment behaves very differently from total employment. Construction leads national growth but shows very low conformity to the nation as a whole.

At actual turning points, construction industries have tended to lead the nation. All construction industries led the nation during the 1974 downturn: general contractors (SIC 15) by 14 months, the others by 7 months; special trade contractors (SIC 17) have consistently led the nation at all upturns since 1960. Although the relationship between the timing of construction sector employment and total employment cycles differs widely across labor market areas, in a majority of labor market areas, construction leads at cycle downturns. There is no strong tendency for a lead at cycle upturn (Vernez et al., 1977). The implication is that the allocation of public works funds should be based on the cyclical behavior of local construction employment, not on total employment.

Construction industries tend to be relatively responsive to changes in the national rate of growth of total employment, although there are considerable differences among different construction industries. General building contractors (SIC 15) experience relatively high cyclical amplitude, above that of total employment, while heavy construction (SIC 16) tends to experience cycles of low amplitude. A countercyclical public works program should concentrate on buildings rather than on heavy construction projects.

Industries that are major suppliers to construction industries, including stone, clay, and glass products (SIC 32), primary and fabricated metals (SICs 33 and 34), and non-electrical equipment (SIC 35) tend to experience severe cycles, are responsive to national changes, and lead cyclical turning points by a few months.

Different occupations reflect cyclical fluctuations with differing amplitude. To some extent, this variation is due to the different distribution of occupations among industries. However, it is doubtful if all differences can be explained in this way. It is probable that an employer would be less willing to release a skilled worker—particularly one with skills which are expensive to develop—in the face of reduced demand than he would an unskilled worker.

Therefore, blue collar workers experience cyclical fluctuations of much greater amplitude than white collar workers. During the recession from 1973 to 1975, all white collar occupation groups experienced an increase in employment, while all blue collar groups experienced a decline. The most dramatic relative amplitudes were with operatives (-12.7 percent) and laborers (-36.9 percent).

The decline in these two categories between 1973 and 1975 totalled more than 3.8 million, more than the net aggregate employment loss of 3.5 million over the same time period.

Young, white males experience the highest increase in unemployment during business cycles. Between 1969 and 1971, the share of total unemployment of white males below the age of 39 rose from 29.1 percent to 36.1 percent.[10] No other group, identified by ethnicity, age, or sex, experienced an increase in its *share* of total unemployment, although all experienced an increase in their *rate* of unemployment.

Much of the variation in unemployment among socioeconomic groups can be explained by differences in the distribution of these groups to different sectors and occupations. When the latter variables were included in a multiple regression analysis,[11] Vernez et al. found that sex and race had little association with cyclical changes in hours worked. For example, while laborers experience high cyclical fluctuations in employment, less than one percent of all females fall into this occupational category, compared with seven percent of all males. The young were the only group significantly affected by business cycles—independent of industrial or occupational affiliation. Age was positively related to hours worked, and the relationship is stronger at cycle trough than at cycle peak.

Unemployment rates for males and females, both white and non-white, fluctuate cyclically. The highest rates, during periods of expansion and contraction, are experienced by females and by non-whites. However, the ratios of female to male unemployment rates by race, and of white to nonwhite unemployment rates by sex, decline during recessions. For example, during 1969, white female unemployment rates were 1.7 times as high as white male unemployment rates. By 1971, this ratio had declined to 1.3.

Changes in the unemployment rates disguise some of the impacts of recessions. Typically, the labor force participation rates of those groups experiencing high average rates of unemployment decline more sharply during recessions than do the participation rates of low unemployment groups. For example, in March 1969, 67.4 percent of the white adult population were employed (Vernez et al., p. 201).

---

10. By comparison, their share of total employment in these years was 29.8 percent and 30.2 percent, respectively.

11. In which "hours worked last week" was the dependent variable.

In March 1971 this had fallen to 66.0 percent, a decline of 1.4 percentage points. Over the same period, the percentage of blacks and other races working declined from 67.3 percent to 65.0 percent, a decline of 2.3 percentage points. There do not appear to be any cyclical differences in the rate of part-time employment by race or sex.

DISTRIBUTION OF JOBS PROVIDED BY COUNTERCYCLICAL GRANTS PROGRAMS

Jobs may be generated in a given industry by a countercyclical program in three ways. First, expenditures may be channeled directly into the sector, where they directly generate employment: public works create jobs directly in the construction sector, and public employment programs generate public sector jobs. Second, the implementation of the programs requires material supplies which create jobs indirectly. Finally, the increased consumption spending by those directly and indirectly provided with jobs, and increased investment spending by businesses facing an expansion of orders, leads to induced employment in consumer goods and investment goods industries.

One-third of the expenditures on public works projects is for on-site construction labor. This is compatible with the relatively large cyclical amplitude of the construction sector. For public service employment programs, almost all the expenditures are directed toward creating jobs in the public sector, which does not exhibit strong cyclical patterns. The success of the latter programs, therefore, depends on the ability to attract the cyclically unemployed from the private sector.

About one-half of the costs of public works projects is for material supplies, although the amount varies considerably.[12] Public works projects make relatively heavy demands for the output of industries whose cyclical changes are of high amplitude. On the other hand, heavy construction projects also draw upon the output of the mining sector (SIC 14), whose low cyclical amplitude is low and therefore raises the possibility of supply constraints.

Patterns of public sector expenditure resulting from a public service employment program are difficult to predict. The local

---

12. See Appendix F, Vernez et al. (1977), for details of the distribution of materials demands among industries for 22 types of projects.

public sector places considerable demands upon the construction sector, particularly for maintenance and repair works—about half as much as actual construction projects per $1000 of expenditure. Public services also demand supplies from the chemicals industry (SIC 28) and the petroleum and related products industry (SIC 29), two industries with low cyclical amplitude. These comparisons are probably misleading, however, since countercyclical public service employment funds are designated for personnel rather than for service delivery.[13] In this case, there will be little demand for materials and services except for the induced effects of increased consumption expenditures.

For each on-site job created, some three jobs are created in industries that supply material or are induced by the spending of salaries (Vernez et al., 1977). It is difficult to estimate the distribution of these jobs in the various sectors. Increased consumer expenditures will be spent predominantly on housing and food.[14]

Over half of those employed in the public sector are professionals, technicians, and service workers, while in the construction sector there is a heavy concentration of craft and kindred workers and unskilled laborers. In general, the public sector draws upon occupations that are not heavily affected by national cyclical downturns, while the construction sector is comprised of occupations that exhibit high cyclical changes.

There is a much higher percentage of professional and technical workers at state government level than at local government level. Conversely, local governments employ a higher concentration of laborers and service workers than state governments do. Neither level of government employs a very high share of craftsmen and operatives.

It is difficult, from these averages, to determine the extent to which a public service employment program could utilize skilled or unskilled labor. The results of two studies are conflicting with respect to the share of new jobs that could be filled by unskilled labor. In 1970 and 1971 the National Civil Service League con-

13. However, if such funds are regarded as substitutes for local funds by local governments, then their net effects on local expenditure may reflect average patterns of disbursements, rather than the labor intensive patterns intended by legislators.

14. Approximately 60 percent of consumption expenditures are for food and housing (Bureau of Labor Statistics, 1976).

ducted interviews with Chicago city personnel administrators and reported that 70 percent of the new jobs available were suitable for unskilled labor, including attendants, assistants, and custodial workers. Levy and Wiseman (1975) investigated needed positions in San Francisco and Oakland limiting their search to existing government slots in the central municipal and educational branches of public service. To assure conservative estimates of demand, they included only those positions which were truly accessible to low-skilled labor.[15] It was found that 21 percent of 3,971 jobs available in Oakland and 16 percent of 24,034 jobs available in San Francisco could use low-skilled workers. Further research from a much broader sample of cities is needed to determine the types of jobs that might be created by a countercyclical Public Service Employment (PSE) program.

The demand for material supplies by public works projects generates jobs in the manufacturing sector which contains a high concentration of operatives and craft workers, two occupational groups that typically experience a high rate of cyclical unemployment.

Countercyclical public service employment programs reach proportionately more males than the manpower programs directed at structural unemployment, although the concentration on male employment by Public Service Employment programs declined slowly over time from 72 percent in 1971–72 to 64 percent in the second quarter of 1976. It remains above the share of males in total unemployment but this is compatible with the fact that males are more affected by cyclical unemployment than females.

Although there are no data available on the sex of participants in countercyclical public works programs, these programs probably target almost exclusively on male labor, which constitutes 95 percent of the labor force in the construction industry and 80 percent in the durable goods industry.

The targeting of countercyclical public service employment and public works programs on the young (aged 21 or less) is not consistent with the relatively high concentration of youth in both total and cyclical unemployment. About one-fifth of the jobs in public

---

15. Levy and Wiseman included only those positions which required a 12th grade or less education and less than 18 months work experience. Jobs posing special union requirements were not counted. Jobs characteristically held by women were eliminated because the study used data from the 1967 Survey of Economic Opportunity (SEO) for males only.

service employment programs go to the young, who represent more than one-third of total unemployment during recessions. Less than 10 percent of the jobs in public works projects are expected to go to youth (Vernez et al., 1977, p. 369). Both the public sector and the construction industry have relatively high job skill and/or experience requirements. To target on youth, a different type of countercyclical program would be required—possibly an expansion during recession of present manpower programs that provide training and other services. Youth is heavily represented in past and present manpower programs.

Workers at the other extreme of the age distribution—45 years and above—have also a lower representation in countercyclical public service employment programs than in total unemployment. But this group is typically less affected by cyclical unemployment. Older workers are well served by public works projects, since they comprise more than a third of the labor force in the construction industry.

Workers with a high school education or more are over-represented in countercyclical public service employment programs. They constitute nearly three-fourths of the participants, but only half of the unemployed. They are also less affected by cyclical unemployment. During the second quarter of FY 1976, nearly 80 percent of new entrants to public service employment under the CETA program were well-educated, because the average education of state and local employees is above that of workers in general. PSE programs provide little or no funds for training or for materials and supplies, which encourages the hiring of those that need the least support services.

Countercyclical programs face an important trade-off between job creation and the provision of training and other supporting services. More than half of cyclical unemployment is the result of a deepening of the unemployment experience of the chronically unemployed—the young and the less educated. Providing jobs for at least half of the cyclically unemployed requires the inclusion of a training component in countercyclical public service employment programs or an expansion of manpower programs during recessionary years.

Countercyclical public works and public service employment programs have provided a high share of jobs for minorities, although to a lesser extent than manpower programs. However, each successive program has provided a smaller share of jobs to minorities —from 40 percent under the original Public Employment Program (PEP) to less than 30 percent under CETA Title VI. The high concentration of minority employment under the Public Works Impact Program is surprising, given that public works projects were built by private contractors and that the proportion of blacks employed in the construction industry is equivalent to that in the total labor forces (about 11 percent). But the program was small and was implemented during expansionary years, when unemployment of whites was relatively low. The extent to which the deliberate set-asides for increased minority participation in construction activity may prove effective is not yet known.

Although countercyclical programs try to provide jobs for the unemployed, up to 30 percent of public service employment participants and 65 percent of PWIP participants were employed on the day prior to program entry.[16] Prior employment by an enrollee does not necessarily mean that a new job has not been created; since the job the enrollee has left may be less attractive than the new one and will be filled by another person. Although net job creation is not altered, the vacated job may not be filled immediately. Also, the enrollee might have become unemployed had he or she not enrolled in the program. A minimum unemployment duration requirement for eligibility is not critical to the issue of job creation, but is critical to issues of equity, search costs for the employer, speed of job creation, and eligibility enforcement. The longer duration of the required unemployment, the slower the process of job creation will be. The requirement will serve to spread the personal cost of job search among a larger group of workers. Of those that were unemployed at entry to CETA public employment programs in calendar year 1975, a majority—58 percent—had been unemployed for 13 weeks or less (Westat 1976).

There is also evidence that countercyclical programs draw a number of participants who were not in the labor force on the day prior to program entry. There is however no information to indicate

---

16. There is scarcity of data indicated whether those employed immediately prior to program entry were working part-time. One study (Westat 1976) indicates that 75 percent of CETA public service employment enrollees in calendar year 1975 that were so employed had been working 36 hours or more a week prior to enrollment (pp. 6–24).

whether these enrollees are new entrants or re-entrants to the labor force.

Conclusions

Two targeting issues were raised at the beginning of this paper—addressing local cyclical needs and providing jobs for those workers most affected either by a countercyclical public works program or a countercyclical public service employment program. Although from area to area there are wide variations in the severity and timing of recessions, there are few consistent patterns from cycle to cycle that would allow the development of an effective allocation formula. A weak case can be made for focusing upon relatively large labor market areas and areas located in the old manufacturing belt.

Public works projects do concentrate their employment impacts on the construction and durable manufacturing sectors, sectors that typically experience cycles of above average severity. However, cyclical patterns of construction employment do not correspond closely with those of the nation as a whole, and by distributing grants on the basis of total unemployment, the federal government runs the risk of encountering constraints in the local availability of construction labor. Projects should also avoid emphasizing heavy construction since this industry does not experience severe cycles. Public works projects do little to provide employment to young workers and to the chronically unemployed, segments of the labor market that bear an especially heavy cyclical burden.

Public employment programs have not focused upon the cyclically unemployed. Targeting could be improved by formulating stricter eligibility requirements and by paying more attention to training and counseling to facilitate job entry by people with a history of frequent unemployment. Overall, both programs have served more to provide countercyclical fiscal relief to jurisdictions whose revenues have suffered as a result of rising unemployment than to recycle job relief. Perhaps they should be evaluated as a politically expedient way of increasing federal fiscal assistance rather than as instruments to stimulate distressed local economies.

REFERENCES

Bureau of Labor Statistics. 1976. *Handbook of Labor Statistics 1976*, Bulletin 1905, U.S. Department of Labor. Washington, D.C.

Levy, Frank, and Wiseman, Michael. 1975. An Expanded Public-Service Employment Program: Some Demand and Supply Considerations. *Public Policy.* vol. 23, no. 1, pp. 105–134.

Peterson, George E. 1976. Finance. In W. Gorham and W. Glazer (eds.), *The Urban Predicament.* Washington, D.C.: The Urban Institute.

Vaughan, Roger. 1976. *Public Works as a Countercyclical Device: A Review of the Issues.* The Rand Corporation, R-1990-EDA.

Vernez, Georges. 1977. *Public Works as Countercyclical Fiscal Policy.* The Rand Corporation, P-5859.

Vernez, Georges, and Vaughan, Roger. 1978. *Assessment of Countercyclical Public Works and Public Service Employment Programs.* The Rand Corporation, R-2214-EDA. Forthcoming.

Vernez, Georges; Vaughan, Roger; Burright, Burke; and Coleman, Sinclair. 1977. *Regional Cycles and Employment Effects of Public Works Investments.* The Rand Corporation, R-2052-EDA.

Westat, Inc. 1976. *Continuous Longitudinal Manpower Survey, Report No. 4.* Prepared for the Office of Policy, Evaluation, and Research, U.S. Department of Labor.

DISCUSSION OF ROGER J. VAUGHAN, "THE USE OF FEDERAL GRANTS FOR COUNTERCYCLICAL JOB CREATION"

George E. Peterson, Discussant

The federal government has a generally acknowledged responsibility for countercyclical management of the national economy. Vaughan's paper considers the appropriate role of grants to state and local governments in federal countercyclical policy. Such grants occupied a much larger part of federal strategy during the last recession than they did in previous economic downturns.

The arguments for relying more heavily upon grants-in-aid as a countercyclical tool have been:

First, the state and local sector is a large part of national economic activity. Left to themselves, state and local governments may fail to support the countercyclical posture of the federal government, or even reinforce national economic cycles through their restrictive budgetary actions. Targeting of countercyclical aid to lower levels of government is said to be desirable as a complement to direct federal fiscal actions.

Second, grants-in-aid provide an opportunity for sharper regional or metropolitan targeting of federal assistance than is possible through uniform national programs. Since regional exposure to national economic fluctuations is greatly variable, this geographical pinpointing is desirable.

Third, skillful design of assistance programs can target countercyclical aid to especially hard hit industries. The Local Public Works program, for example, directed $6 billion of temporary funds to construction and related industries.

162

The desirability of having a strong grant component in federal countercyclical policy depends on the persuasiveness of these rationales.

Public Sector Targeting

Do state and local governments have a special claim on federal succor during times of recession?

The majority of public sector workers are employed in professional and technical occupations or as service workers. These occupational sectors experience considerably below-average exposure to recessionary cycles. Despite some highly publicized layoffs, state and local employees, in particular, have had unusually stable work histories. The use of federal funds to create jobs in state and local governments thus has elements of perverse selectivity. It is possible that new hires for temporary public service employment could be drawn from different, and more cyclically vulnerable, labor pools, but this remains conjecture.

Detailed studies by the Advisory Commission on Intergovernmental Relations and the General Accounting Office have established that during recent recessions the behavior of state and local governments has been mildly countercyclical even in the absence of special federal aid (that is, sector expenditures have continued to rise throughout recessions despite revenue lags). Consequently, federal assistance would not appear to be necessary to avoid perverse state-local spending behavior that would jeopardize national economic recovery.

There is also evidence that a large part of temporary federal aid is captured by recipient governments through substitution for locally financed spending or through accumulation of financial reserves. On the criterion that the best countercyclical program is the one that induces the largest and quickest stimulative bang for the buck, aid to lower levels of governments ranks rather unimpressively on a list of countercyclical policy options.

Despite these reservations, it is possible that the large influx of federal assistance to state and local governments in 1975–77 had a cyclically calming effect. Perhaps the greatest danger to economic instability lay in the transmission of local fiscal crises through the municipal bond market, as cities were cut off from access to borrowing because of their financial positions. The strengthening of local government financial reserves was as important to solid economic recovery as the rebuilding of corporate liquidity. The especially fragile position of local government finances in 1975 may well have warranted special federal assistance, even if job programs were converted by recipients to general assistance programs. Of course, as Vaughan points out, this objective would have been more clearly served by having a single program of countercyclical revenue sharing.

Geographical Targeting

Virtually all federal countercyclical programs carry with them geographical targeting. Unemployment payments, for example, are automatically targeted to areas having the greatest collections of unemployed persons. Is there a convincing rationale for additional targeting?

The public interest that brings countercyclical assistance into focus presumably comes from the agglomeration effects of unemployment. Though a cyclically unemployed person in Austin, Texas, may be no more distressed than a cyclically unemployed person in Detroit, his chances of finding a job during a recession probably are better; moreover, the concentration of unemployment has repercussions on the local tax base that spread the effects of recession more widely among the populace. Whether these geographical effects justify anything more than uniform payments to all unemployed persons or national efforts at job creation (which automatically target their benefits to high unemployment areas) is unclear. Discussants were skeptical that there was a persuasive rationale for the kind of geographical targeting found in the public service employment and local public works programs.

It was also questioned whether geographical targeting through local public works (LPW) was feasible. Evidence cited by Vaughan indicates that most of the net employment effect of LPW comes from the backward linkages of demand for capital goods and materials. More than 90 percent of these second-round jobs are located outside of the labor market of initial investment. They tend to be concentrated in areas where capital goods producers and other industrial suppliers to the construction industry are located. Thus the original targeting of aid tends to be offset by subsequent dispersion of induced employment.

Industry Targeting

Local public works programs frequently are justified in preference to other countercyclical programs because they direct their principal benefits to high unemployment industries, like construction and capital goods.

Discussants pointed out that federal unemployment payments already single out cyclical industries for special federal assistance, and that hourly wages in construction and capital goods production are higher than in other industries because of the expectation of less stable employment. It was questioned whether further favorable treatment of these industries was in order.

The operation of the local public works program would appear to mute several of the private market incentives to employment recovery in the construction industry. The requirement that Davis-Bacon wages be paid to construction workers in LPW projects has the effect of preventing construction wages from falling as far as they otherwise would. According to some LPW evaluations, construction workers prefer to work part time in the public sector at higher wages rather than work longer periods in the private sector at recession-induced lower wages. The net result is to have federally funded local public construction substitute, in part, for private construction.

Are the Programs Countercyclical? Should They Be?

Though the aid programs in the Economic Stimulus Package were described as countercyclical, funds were disbursed according to total local unemployment rates, not the cyclical component of unemployment rates. As Vaughan shows, this produced gross inequalities in federal payments per cyclically unemployed worker. Like many other commentators, Vaughan faults the countercyclical grant programs for muddling cyclical and structural employment objectives.

Such criticisms may give too great importance to program labels and exaggerate the virtues of singlemindedness in public policy. The economic stimulus grants proceeded from a perception of the inadequacies of national economic stimulation in restoring acceptable unemployment levels in all parts of the country. In part, this was due to regional variations in the intensity of cyclical downturns. In at least equal part, however, differentiated grants-in-aid were inspired by the belief that there were regional immobilities of factor supply—particularly regional pools of unemployed labor—which could best be absorbed by regionally targeted demand.

The "temporary" public employment policies reviewed in this paper now become the base for permanent public service employment, also highly targeted by local and regional unemployment rates. It seems unduly restrictive to evaluate them as if they were solely intended to be what their labels announced: countercyclical programs. They were, rather, structural programs introduced with the language that made them most politically acceptable in 1975–76, that of combating a temporary recession. They now require evaluation for their impact upon structural unemployment rates.